Aquinas, Science,
and Human Uniqueness

Aquinas, Science, and Human Uniqueness

An Integrated Approach to the Question
of What Makes Us Human

Mary L. Vanden Berg

CASCADE *Books* · Eugene, Oregon

AQUINAS, SCIENCE, AND HUMAN UNIQUENESS
An Integrated Approach to the Question of What Makes Us Human

Cascade Books
An imprint of Wipf and Stock Publishers
199 W. 8th Ave., Suite 3
Eugene, OR 97401

www.wipfandstock.com

PAPERBACK ISBN: 978-1-7252-6777-0
HARDCOVER ISBN: 978-1-7252-6776-3
EBOOK ISBN: 978-1-7252-6778-7

Cataloguing-in-Publication data:

Names: Vanden Berg, Mary L. [author].

Title: Aquinas, science, and human uniqueness : an integrated approach to the question of what makes us human / Mary L. Vanden Berg.

Description: Eugene, OR: Cascade Books, 2022 | Includes bibliographical references.

Identifiers: ISBN 978-1-7252-6777-0 (paperback) | ISBN 978-1-7252-6776-3 (hardcover) | ISBN 978-1-7252-6778-7 (ebook)

Subjects: LCSH: Thomas, Aquinas, Saint, 1225?–1274 | Theological anthropology—Christianity | Religion and science | Human evolution—Religious aspects—Christianity

Classification: BT701.3 V36 2022 (print) | BT701.3 (ebook)

For my Dad, Wilbur, my sister, Judy, and my friend's son, David, who are now at home with the Lord, and who through their challenges have challenged me to consider more deeply what it is to be human.

Contents

Acknowledgements

I WANT TO BEGIN by thanking the Henry Center at Trinity Evangelical Divinity School, whose gift of a fellowship with the Templeton-funded Creation Project inspired my thinking on this topic. I am especially grateful for ideas and suggestions during that time from my colleagues Ryan Peterson, Dru Johnson, Geoffrey Fulkerson, James Hoffmeier, and Bradley Gundlach, as well as many conversations with Joel Chopp on Aquinas.

I also want to thank Calvin Theological Seminary for granting me a semester leave at the Creation Project and a sabbatical to finish up my research on this work. The support of my administrators, both on this project and in my general duties as a professor, is exemplary and much appreciated. In addition, I want to thank the many colleagues and friends willing to engage my ideas and read through chapters or parts of chapters over the past year. In particular, I owe special thanks to Dr. Ryan Bebej, Dr. Clay Carlson, Dr. John Hilber, and Dr. Ralph Stearley. Thank you also to my research assistant, Ruan Bessa da Silva, whose diligent work helping me find resources, reading through chapters, making suggestions, and offering a non-North American perspective on a variety of issues was a constant blessing. I would also like to thank my copy editor, J. Andrew Edwards, whose advise and suggestions on my manuscript draft enhanced the quality of the final product.

My husband deserves special thanks for his tireless support of my research, teaching, and writing over the past number of years. Forty years ago, neither of us expected that God would lead me to this particular vocation. It took some adjustment for both of us but I know I would not be where I am today without his love and constant encouragement. And, of course, his support of me is multiplied by that of our children—Charlie, Rachel, Peter, Ashley, Michelle, and Jordan. Each of you has challenged me to think outside of my box in so many ways. Thank you for always being willing to make me think harder than almost anyone else about how "normal people" think. I love you all so very much and am so grateful for your love. That God gave me each of you is more than I could have ever hoped for. That he has now allowed me to see my children's children is an added blessing.

Most of all, I am grateful to the Triune God, who in Christ by the power of the Holy Spirit led me to himself, claimed me as his own, called me to this work, and daily gives me "good confidence that nothing will separate me from his love." May these meditations be pleasing to you, O God, my rock and my salvation. *Soli Deo Gloria.*

Introduction

WHAT IS A HUMAN? This self-reflective question has been around for millennia and has had multiple answers. Are we, as some would suggest, the product of millions of years of chance mutations and changes, randomly ordered organic material? Or perhaps we are simply tailless monkeys, hairless apes not really that different from the rest of the animal kingdom. Are the ancient hominids that have been unearthed in recent decades human? How would we know? What marks out humans as unique—or aren't humans unique after all?

On a general level, most people would agree that humans are unique. More precisely, there would be agreement that humans have unique features that identify them as part of the group of creatures known as *homo sapiens*. For example, they might observe that no other creature has the ability to speak, so speech is uniquely human. This is not to say that no other animals communicate, only that they do not speak with all that speech entails. But of course, other animals have features that are unique to them. Only elephants have tusks and trunks, for example. So to say that humans are unique really isn't saying much. The more important question is "*How are humans unique?*" What sets humans apart from other living beings? Or put another way, What makes humans *special*?

Some might argue that although humans are unique in the general sense, we aren't actually all that special. They might note that humans share a lot of characteristics with other mammals. We know, for example, that humans share something close to 98.7 percent of their genome with chimpanzees.[1] Indeed, according to David Wilcox, "Chimpanzee DNA is closer to human DNA than to gorilla DNA."[2] At a more obvious level, a trip to a museum will make clear that the skeletal structure of humans, chimps, and

---

1. Wilcox, "Our Genetic Prehistory." Also Jeffrey Norris, "What Makes Us Human?"
2. Wilcox, "Our Genetic Prehistory," 83.

1

various gorillas is also fairly similar. But similarities do not end with the merely physical. Oliver Putz draws on a wide range of scientific studies to argue that the great apes can be understood as moral beings and, therefore, should be included with humans as bearing the image of God.[3]

In a slightly different vein, Keri McFarlane observes that humans are one of many species (*homo sapiens*) within the kingdom *animalia*. She goes on to point out that distinctions between species are not as clear cut as we might think. She notes "an attempt to define the differences between humans and nonhumans is proving difficult, as our understanding of distinctive criteria continues to shift in the light of ethological scientific advancements."[4] Her overarching concern is the humane treatment of animals, asserting at one point that considering humans as special carries the risk of "an "us and them" mentality" that could increase animal suffering.[5]

McFarlane's worry is shared by any number of people ranging from activist groups to theologians and philosophers. These groups emphasize the similarities between species, while also rejecting any sort of hierarchy between human animals and the rest of the animal kingdom. Some even refer to those who affirm a hierarchy as engaging in "speciesism." Along with this notion of speciesism is the idea that humans, as animals, differ from other animals only in degree, not in kind. Jim Stump writes that Darwin himself asserted this idea, an assertion that Stump suggests implies "we're nothing but animals that have learned a few new tricks."[6] The overarching worry for those who argue against this speciesism is that affirming a hierarchy could lead to animal cruelty or even the degradation of creation as a whole.[7] This sort of general thinking lies behind many other works on animal rights and animal welfare.

---

3. Putz, "Moral Apes, Human Uniqueness, and the Image of God."

4. McFarlane, "Living Relationally," 235.

5. McFarlane, "Living Relationally," 237.

6. Jim Stump, "Scientific Testimonies to Human Uniqueness," BioLogos (blog), May 21, 2018, https://biologos.org/post/scientific-testimonies-to-human-uniqueness/. For a more extensive description of Darwin's beliefs on this matter, see Van Huyssteen, *Alone in the World?* 69–75.

7. See, for example, the seminal work edited by Peter Singer, *In Defense of Animals*; on a cultural level, see PETA, https://www.peta.org/about-peta/. Similarly, Tom Regan argues that there is no "morally relevant difference between all humans and other animals." Regan, "Moral Basis of Vegetarianism." See also Linzey, "Theological Basis of Animal Rights"; Linzey, *Christianity and Rights*; Bekoff and Colin, "Deep Ethology."

On the one hand, arguments regarding animal welfare deserve consideration from the perspective of what Christian stewardship of creation should look like. On the other hand, it is not clear that the suggestion that humans are special *necessarily* leads to the misuse of creation, whether that misuse has to do only with animals or with creation as a whole. On a purely anecdotal level, most people are neither vegetarian nor members of PETA, regardless of whether they are concerned with animal welfare. Many people do, however, consider humans special in a variety of ways. Everything from the global concern for human rights, as illustrated in documents like those produced by the United Nations,[8] to the elaborate funeral practices and mourning rituals found in most cultures signal that humans are generally understood as special and deserving of special concern. The more common problem with respect to understanding humans as special is not *whether* they are special in general, but rather whether some particular group of humans actually counts as human and therefore deserves the concomitant dignity that goes with being human.

Although the impact of questions regarding who counts as human and who does not is fairly common knowledge, it is worth mentioning here if only to point out a potential problem with belief systems that aim to affirm the equal value of humans and other animals: namely, that while aiming to elevate the status of non-human animals, they often simultaneously end up diminishing the value of humans. In my context in the United States, the practice of chattel slavery followed by Jim Crow laws and other less observable practices had at their root the idea that the color of one's skin rendered one somehow less than human. Along those same lines, the native people groups that European settlers encountered were frequently referred to with adjectives like "savage" and treated accordingly. The roots of this may have been in theories of "pre-Adamites," theories that developed in part as a way to make sense of various races that Europeans encountered as they explored the world.[9] Outside of the United States, Nazi Germany offers another example of dehumanization. Under Adolf Hitler's Nazi regime, Jews, Gypsies, the disabled, and other people were considered less than human and thus could be used for experimentation and, in general, treated as less than human. Likewise in India, the lives of the Dalit are considered

8. United Nations, "Universal Declaration of Human Rights," https://www.un.org/en/about-us/universal-declaration-of-human-rights/.

9. The theory of the pre-Adamites was also connected to the theory of evolution and the discovery of hominids that suggested an early date for the earth. For more on this see David N. Livingstone's excellent work, *Adam's Ancestors*.

less valuable than that of certain animals. Unfortunately, this sort of thing is not unusual in human history, and it seems unlikely that any given model of what it means to be human will eliminate our tendency to dehumanize those who are different than the dominant group.

Marguerite Shuster sums up the problem of dehumanization well in a sermon entitled "Who Are We?" Commenting on the question of Psalm 8, "What is man that you are mindful of him, the son of man that you care for him?" she notes that the question is based "on a keen sense of humankind's frailness, impotence, and mortality, compared to the power and expanse of creation."[10] She thinks this question of human significance is even more pronounced for us than for the psalmist given what we know about the universe. She compares human smallness to the vastness of the universe, human weakness to the strength of the elephant. She then asks, "So what's so special about us?" She insightfully answers:

> It matters, profoundly, how we answer that question; because if, in false humility, we say, "nothing," we will do terrible evil. If we say that, obviously enough, we are simply animals and not very impressive animals at that, we will surely act like animals. Similarly but more chillingly, Abraham Heschel suggests that there may be a connection between believing that one is simply made up of enough "fat to make seven cakes of soap, enough iron to make a medium sized nail," and so on; and "what the Nazis actually did in the extermination camps: make soap out of human flesh." Rob human beings of their unique dignity, and we will treat them as beasts or objects. Again, then, it matters that we take a proper view of ourselves, and therefore of other human selves, because what we believe makes a difference in how we behave.[11]

If human history is any gauge of the truth, Shuster appears to be right. While there may be evolutionary reasons for the human propensity to distrust those unlike themselves, reducing the "other" to something less than human—a mere animal—opens a door to unspeakable horrors.

The Christian church has historically responded to the question of whether humans are unique using the story of Scripture as its starting point. Scripture offers a picture of humans that sets them both *apart from* and *above* the rest of creation. Within the created order, humans are the crown of creation. This teaching is drawn from Scripture as a whole, but

10. Shuster, "Who Are We?" 13.
11. Shuster, "Who Are We?" 13–14.

most often it centers on the creation story as recorded in Genesis 1. In this story, humans and humans alone are said to be created *in the image of God:* "So God created man in his own image, in the image of God he created him; male and female he created them" (Gen 1:27). What precisely this text means has been the subject of much debate.

Most biblical scholars suggest that the best interpretation of the image as described in this text is *functional*—that is, they emphasize the assigned role (or function) of humans as rulers over creation.[12] Other theologians suggest that a *relational* view takes better account of the I-Thou relation between God and humanity, and the nature of humans as relational, communal beings. Such a view reflects the Christian perspective of God as living in eternal, tri-personal relationship.[13] It is, in other words, in and through our relationality, they suggest, that humans image God. These more recent views intentionally move away from an older, premodern understanding of the image of God as intellective. The intellective view of the image of God considers humans as most like God in our ability to know and love God, something analogous to how God knows and loves us.

The understanding of humans as intellective beings has been criticized as relying too heavily on the intellect as the *sole* capacity that marks out humans as unique from other creatures. Premodern models do seem, at least at times, to be guilty of defining humans generally (or the *imago Dei* in particular) solely in terms of intellectual capability to the detriment of other aspects of human experience. The criticism has run the gamut from suggestions that the heavy emphasis of the Christian tradition on the intellect is overly dependent on Greek philosophy to suggesting that an emphasis on intellect has stifled healthy emotional expression. In addition, some have described the potential of these older models to marginalize certain people, particularly those with intellectual disabilities.[14] These are

12. For example, Middleton, *Liberating Image*, 30–34. See also Wenham, *Genesis 1–15*, 30–33; Niskanen, "Poetics of Adam," 430, 433. See also Herring, "'Transubstantiated' Humanity," 480.

13. Plantinga, "Images of God," 59–63; Barth, *Church Dogmatics* 3/1, 49–50, 363–64.; LaCugna, *God for Us*; Grenz, *Social God and Relational Self*; Viazovski, *Image and Hope*, 165–69; Swinton, *Dementia*, 148.

14. See for example, Cortez, *Theological Anthropology*, 18–29; Van der Kooi and Van den Brink, *Christian Dogmatics*, 261–62; Kärkkäinen, *Creation and Humanity*, 274–75; Reinders, *Receiving the Gift*, 1, 89. It may also be worth mentioning that the modern philosophical and theological bias against any form of substance metaphysics is also likely part of the root of dispensing with intellective models, most of which are linked to older metaphysical sensibilities.

important concerns, but they overlook the fact that, from a biological/neuropsychological point of view, function and relationality are also dependent on intellective capacity.[15]

It is also important to note that the way some premodern theologians like Thomas Aquinas understand a term like "intellective capacity," and how they locate that capacity is very different from modern ways of thinking about intellect. Modern theology tends to use and understand "intellective capacity" in ways more closely linked to modern science and materialism than the Aristotelian metaphysics in which this term was rooted for someone like Aquinas. Thus, depending on how "intellective capacity" is defined, maybe the premodern impulse to identify the intellect as an important and unique feature of humans is not as far off-base as might be thought. Rather, it could comport fairly well with general observations of human persons as a whole. Regardless of how one parses out exactly what it means that humans are made in the image of God, however, the Christian tradition as a whole has asserted what Scripture portrays overall—that humans, for any number of reasons, are different from other animals, not just in *degree*, but in *kind*. Humans, to borrow a term from Gijsbert van den Brink's insightful book, are "specially unique," a reference to what he describes as "the specific form of uniqueness that makes us radically different from all other species and more special and precious than them."[16]

That is what I will affirm and expand upon in this book. Drawing on Scripture, science, and St. Thomas Aquinas, I will argue that humans are specially unique because they are complex material-spiritual, intellective, worshipping beings, specially created this way by God with the ultimate purpose—the *telos*—of knowing and loving God. Indeed, human flourishing in this life is dependent upon a human orientation toward this loving relationship with God.[17] I will show that this description, which includes a retrieval and affirmation of human intellective capacity, is not only a legitimate description, but one that encompasses *all* humans, from a tiny human embryo and a newborn baby, to those born with an intellectual disability, to a person who suffers a catastrophic brain injury, and to a person like

15. By saying that relationality and function are intertwined with intellect is simply to acknowledge that most of what we do as humans cannot be easily isolated into only one area of the brain, given what we know about how humans actually process operations. Relationality and intellect are intimately connected to the point that so-called social intelligence may be a better indicator of success overall than standard IQ tests.

16. Van den Brink, *Reformed Theology and Evolutionary Theory*, 143.

17. Ortiz, *You Made Us*, 31.

my father who was intellectually challenged due to advanced dementia. In other words, riffing off of Christian Smith, humans are material-spiritual, intellective, worshipping animals.[18] Any one of these characteristics by itself may not set humans apart from other animals, but the combination of all of these—a combination shared by *all* humans—mark *homo sapiens* as specially unique.

I will begin with an exposition of Aquinas's Treatise on Human Nature—that is, questions 75–102 in the first part (*prima pars*) of the *Summa Theologiae*. Although Aquinas has been the subject of much theological and philosophical reflection in Roman Catholic circles, many Protestant theologians are unfamiliar with Aquinas and his thinking. The frequent misunderstandings and misportrayals of Aquinas's thought are sufficient to warrant the time and space it takes to describe him. Furthermore, much of the work that Protestants have done on Aquinas focuses on his treatment of God and virtue ethics, but not as much has been written by way of exposition on the Treatise on Human Nature. This chapter, therefore, will offer an introduction to Aquinas as well as a description of this important part of his work. Aquinas suggests a number of ways that humans are unique, distinct from the rest of creation. First, only humans are made immediately by God. Second, only humans have a physical body and an intellective soul. Third, only humans are made in the image of God. And fourth, only humans survive death. Finally, along with most of the Western tradition, Aquinas recognizes humans as teleological beings whose ultimate purpose (*telos*) is to know and love God. I will argue that a retrieval of this holistic framework of thinking about humans can offer a helpful inroad to discussions about what marks out humans as specially unique.

The second chapter will focus on biblical evidence for humans as specially unique within creation, paying particular attention to the grammatical-historical-literary structure of Genesis 1 and 2. A close reading of these biblically foundational chapters will offer a window into details of the text that emphasize both the unique creation of the first humans as compared to the rest of creation and the special vocation of humanity. In addition, I will draw on selections from the Psalms and wisdom literature to offer a more complete biblical account of human persons that includes, but is not limited to, discussions of the image of God.

---

18. I have been helpfully shaped in my thinking about humans by Christian Smith's work, especially his anthropology, *Moral, Believing Animals*.

The third chapter will examine the current scientific evidence that the human genome and various anatomical and behavioral aspects of humans are both strikingly similar to but also radically different from other creatures. This chapter will examine not only the breadth of our similarity to other creatures, but also the depth of our differences. I will suggest that the scientific evidence is at best inconclusive for determining whether humans differ from other creatures not just in degree, but in kind. At the same time, I will posit that the physical evidence does point to enough difference between the traits of humans and even our nearest evolutionary relatives to suggest that humans are, in fact, specially unique within the physical creation.

Having taken a look at both the biblical and scientific evidence for humans as unique beings, the fourth chapter will digress from the central question of human uniqueness to offer some insight into how best to understand these two sources, including where the priority must lie in questions like human uniqueness. Quite often, both scientists and theologians are inclined to try to reconcile or harmonize these two sources when differences arise. This primarily pastoral chapter will suggest that harmonization is not always the best answer, especially for persons sitting in our churches. I will suggest that while harmonization may be appropriate for some persons who are seeking understanding, for others we should consider treating these two sources as two stories that intersect at points. Where fundamental differences arise, we should affirm the authority of Scripture while allowing the difference under consideration to be understood as an apparent paradox and encourage people to live with the tension between the stories rather than trying to accommodate one story to the other.

The fifth chapter will bring together the insights drawn from Aquinas, Scripture, and science to propose how exactly humans are specially unique. Drawing on the work of the previous four chapters along with reaching into the deep wells of the broad theological tradition, this constructive chapter will offer an understanding of humans persons as complex material-spiritual, intellective, worshipping beings designed by God for the ultimate purpose of knowing and loving God, a love that naturally expresses itself in worship. I will argue here that it is precisely this teleological complex that make humans specially unique. The special uniqueness of humans is both a status and a calling that not only sets humans apart as the crown of creation, but also confers responsibility for the rest of creation.

After a brief summary, the sixth and concluding chapter will offer a few thoughts on the potential implications of our "special uniqueness" for ministry. What sorts of actions and behaviors and attitudes should the church foster if we want to fully embrace the majesty of humans as specially unique, as presented in Scripture and the theological tradition? In particular, I will consider the importance for the church of affirming the dignity of *all* humans, particularly those at the edges of life, the reality of human fellowship with God after death, and the connection between worship of the one true God and human *telos*.

1

Aquinas's Anthropology

MY STARTING POINT FOR the discussion about what makes humans unique among other creatures and why this matters is the writing of Thomas Aquinas. In particular, this chapter will focus most of its energy on Aquinas's Treatise on Human Nature, found toward the end of the first part of his *Summa Theologiae*, although at times I will draw on some of his other writings. But this leads to a question: why Aquinas? To put it another way, why would I, a confessionally Reformed theologian, choose Aquinas to offer a foundation for my argument that humans are material-spiritual, intellective, worshipping animals? Why not someone from within my own tradition—someone like Turretin, Bavinck, or Barth? Or maybe more importantly, why not begin the discussion with Scripture?

There are several reasons. The first reason for choosing Aquinas is his *precision* as a theologian. Aquinas's anthropology, especially his Treatise on Human Nature, is clear, precise, and comprehensive, synthesizing biblical and philosophical reflections to elucidate how, from a Christian point of view, humans ought to be understood. His scholastic love for making fine distinctions adds to the precision and helps clearly elucidate what distinguishes humans from the rest of creation. Specifically, Aquinas believes that humans *are* specially unique within creation, which, for the purposes of this study, makes him an apt choice. The fact that Aquinas has a substantive view of human persons that focuses on the intellect as central to what it means to be a human makes the choice even more compelling, given the general distaste in theology not only for substantive models of the image of God, but also for descriptions like Aquinas's that suggest human persons—all of us—are intellectual/rational beings.

Secondly, plenty of Protestant theologians have focused their theological anthropology on prominent figures in the Reformed tradition. This is particularly true of various works that build on Barth, both in Reformed studies and Protestant theology in general. However, there is relatively little written on Aquinas in these circles.[1] This is despite the fact that Aquinas's thinking is clearly in the purview of early Reformed thinkers like John Calvin, John Owen, and Herman Bavinck—and despite the abundance of writing on his anthropology in Roman Catholic theology, as well as within the field of philosophical theology more generally. In addition, much of what has been written in Protestant theology has misunderstood Aquinas and described his thinking in ways that he himself would not recognize.[2] While my argument for Aquinas's depiction of humans may not be satisfying to his detractors, I hope that they nonetheless gain greater understanding of what he actually teaches, particularly with regard to his description of the intellectual capacity of humans.

Finally, a retrieval of Aquinas's biblical and theological understanding of human persons and their place in the created order offers a rich template for interacting with both the biblical text and scientific sources in order to build a cogent theological picture of humans. As will be shown below, Aquinas, like the majority of premodern theologians, does not have a sharp divide between theology and exegesis. Rather, he reads Scripture theologically, apart from more modern assumptions that often result in both the suggestion that grammatical and historical concerns virtually exhaust the meaning of any given text and a text being isolated from the larger canon of Scripture that has been received by the church.[3]

1. For example, Grenz, *Social God and Relational Self*; Cortez, *Theological Anthropology*. In addition, a recent excellent comprehensive volume on Christian dogmatics in the Reformed tradition makes no mention of Aquinas at all in their chapter on theological anthropology: Van der Kooi and Van den Brink, *Christian Dogmatics*.

2. See for example, Reinders, *Receiving the Gift*. In chapter 3, Reinders offers a description of the "Roman Catholic" doctrine of being human, based on the "Aristotelian-Thomistic" traditions. Unfortunately, much of what Reinders offers here is a distortion of the nuances of the Roman Catholic position as well as a misunderstanding of Aquinas and his use of Aristotle.

3. For more on this, see Treier, *Introducing Theological Interpretation*.

Aquinas the Theologian

One of the questions that arises when working with Aquinas has to do with his method, particularly his frequent use of philosophy. The fact that Aquinas's work is often the subject of philosophical study might even make one wonder whether relying on him as a theologian is a legitimate avenue to follow. While it is the case that some scholarship focuses on Aquinas as a philosopher, tending to ignore Aquinas the theologian, it is important to realize that he was as much a theologian as a philosopher. The tendency to emphasize Aquinas the philosopher is largely due to a misunderstanding of his method.[4] The accepted method of his time took full account of philosophy, including the study of Aristotelian physics and metaphysics, along with biblical exegesis. Recognizing this synthesis in his work, Eleonore Stump writes that the *ST* "is the paradigm of philosophical theology."[5] It is a melding of natural—that is, metaphysical—and revealed theology, the ultimate subject of which is God. "Thus," writes Stump, "some of the work of philosophical theology is an attempt to explain revealed propositions [Scripture] and systematically work out their implications."[6] This is not unlike the discipline of systematic theology today. In systematic theology, we faithfully exegete Scripture, exposing various revealed ideas and propositions. We also use the tools of philosophy and logic to unpack what we have found, seeking understanding of these revealed ideas and sewing them together in a way that shows an inherent and organic cohesiveness.[7]

Along these same lines, Matthew Levering has pointed out that for Aquinas, rather than being opposed to scriptural reflection, metaphysics was seen as a way "of deepening our contemplative union with the living God revealed in Scripture."[8] In other words, philosophical reflection went hand in hand with biblical faith as one means for enriching one's meditation on God. Indeed, a "contemplative orientation" is a hallmark of Aquinas's work.[9] And while Aquinas's metaphysics is primarily Aristotelian,

---

4. See, for example, Oliphant, *Thomas Aquinas*, as well as Richard A. Müller's critical review of this work, "Reading Aquinas."

5. Stump, *Aquinas*, 29.

6. Stump, *Aquinas*, 31.

7. Examples of this method in Reformed theology are numerous. Two contemporary examples are Van den Brink and Van der Kooi, *Christian Dogmatics*, and Michael Horton, *Christian Faith*.

8. Levering, *Scripture and Metaphysics*, 2.

9. Torrell, *Aquinas's Summa*, 1, 20.

this is not to say that he simply takes over Aristotle's ideas uncritically. It is clear in various places in the *ST* not only that he disagrees with Aristotle at times, but also that when Aristotle conflicts with Scripture, Scripture as revealed knowledge has the upper hand. In other words, philosophy is a tool for faith seeking understanding, but it is not the ultimate source of theology—as is clear in the very first question of the *ST*. Torrell writes that Aquinas "was first and foremost a commentator of Sacred Scripture and a theologian who took pains to explain the doctrines of the faith."[10] Thus, any criticisms that Aquinas is not biblically rooted or is too Greek in his ideas reflect ignorance of his basic method of working with truth wherever he finds it, while at the same time giving preference to revealed truth when there are sticking points.

DeYoung, McCloskey, and Van Dyke offer a helpful description of this cross-fertilization of Aristotle and Christian belief in Aquinas's method. They write that "one of the most striking features of Aquinas's scholarship is its conscious synthesis of Aristotelian philosophy with his Christian beliefs."[11] It is good to emphasize again that Aquinas's method is no bare appropriation of Aristotle, a "baptizing" of Aristotle's thought. DeYoung et al. insist that Aquinas's "theological commitments permeate his philosophical system."[12] Aquinas's method, in other words, is an unashamedly Christian theological method that uses the tools of reason to elucidate and explicate revealed knowledge.[13]

In the opening of the *ST*, Thomas argues for both the primacy and the necessity of revealed truths, truths that are not accessible to philosophical reasoning.[14] He is not arguing that philosophical reasoning is bad, only that it is incomplete. Commenting on 2 Timothy 3:16, he writes, "Now Scripture, inspired of God, is no part of philosophical science, which has been built up by human reason. Therefore it is useful that besides philosophical science, there should be other knowledge, i.e. inspired of God."[15] He goes on to argue that this "other knowledge" is divinely revealed and is necessary for salvation. These revealed truths "exceed reason." He writes, "In order

10. Torrell, *Aquinas's Summa*, 5.

11. DeYoung et al., *Aquinas's Ethics*, 4.

12. DeYoung et al., *Aquinas's Ethics*, 4.

13. Question 1 in the *Summa Theologiae* affirms this as well. There Aquinas notes that the subject of sacred doctrine is God as revealed.

14. Aquinas, *ST* Ia, q. 1, art. 1, s.c.

15. Aquinas, *ST* Ia, q. 1, art. 1, s.c.

that the salvation of men might be brought about more fitly and surely, it was necessary that they should be taught divine truths by divine revelation. It was therefore necessary that besides philosophical science built up by reason, there should be sacred science learned through revelation."[16] Commenting on the conflict between those who read Aquinas as a philosopher and those who read him as a theologian, Frederick Christian Bauerschmidt writes that to understand Aquinas properly, "one must see [the *ST*] as a whole in which philosophical moments are integrated into the pursuit of the truth of the God revealed in Jesus Christ."[17] Likewise, John O'Callaghan, commenting on Aquinas's method notes that, like Augustine, Aquinas proceeds from God to creation. He explains, "The rational movement from God as revealed to creatures in the light of that revelation is the method of theology according to St. Thomas, in contrast to the method of philosophy that proceeds from creatures to God and does not rely upon revelation but employs unaided reason."[18] Thus, reading Aquinas as a theologian while recognizing his philosophical acuity seems not only to be true to his method, but also to affirm how Aquinas saw himself and his project in the *ST*.

One other criticism that is frequently raised against Aquinas is that his complex theological anthropology is too abstract.[19] There is no denying that Aquinas's approach is highly abstract, but no more so than many contemporary philosophical and theological anthropologies. It is unclear to this author why a high level of abstraction is reason to dismiss one of the greatest thinkers in Christian history. This critique also fails to understand that the *ST* was likely written for the educational formation of Dominican friars.[20] It is indeed the case that Aquinas does not bring into his argumentation many concrete examples to help elucidate the abstract concepts he proposes. But as Bauerschmidt points out, this simply leaves the task of finding or creating examples to the reader.[21]

16. Aquinas, *ST* Ia, q.1, art. 1, co. It is worth pointing out here that Aquinas likely understands both holy Scripture (*sacra scriptura*) and holy teaching (*sacra doctrina*) as associated with divine revelation. For more on this see Valkenberg, "Scripture," 51–54.

17. Bauerschmidt, "Reading the *Summa*," 22.

18. O'Callaghan, "*Imago Dei*," 108.

19. For example, Cortez, *Theological Anthropology*, 20.

20. Bauerschmidt, "Reading the *Summa*," 18.

21. Bauerschmidt, "Reading the *Summa*," 15.

Introduction to the Treatise on Human Nature

Aquinas's Treatise on Human Nature is one example of the sort of integrative theological work described above. Aquinas was a member of the Order of Preachers, or Dominicans. His primary task as a "master of the biblical sciences" was threefold, as Torrell explains: "*legere* to read, that is to comment on Scripture by means of teaching; *disputare* to dispute, that is, to engage in a kind of teaching that involved responding to objections on a given theme; and *praedicare* or preaching, that is, to explain Sacred Scripture to a broader audience."[22] Aquinas makes clear in the prologue that his purpose for writing the *ST* was to teach "beginners" in theology. "Because the doctor of Catholic truth ought not only to teach the most advanced but also instruct beginners . . . we purpose in this book to treat of whatever belongs to the Christian religion in such a way as may tend to the instruction of beginners."[23]

The overall organizational structure of the *ST* is tripartite. Torrell writes that in the *ST*, Aquinas "will speak first of God (I), then of movement of the rational creature to God (II), and finally of Christ, who in his humanity, is the way that leads to God (III)."[24] Aquinas deals with humanity, the Treatise on Human Nature, under the general category of the works of God therefore, as part of the first section.

As one of the works of God, humans come after Aquinas's discussion of angels and in the context of his discussion of the six days of creation. Aquinas begins the Treatise on Human Nature (*ST* I, qq. 75–102) with what may at first glance seem to be a philosophical discussion of human persons.[25] Although direct biblical quotes are not plentiful in this section, one should not too quickly dismiss the role of Scripture in Aquinas's thinking. Pim Valkenberg notes that the number of biblical quotations or references is not a good measure of the biblical influence present in Aquinas's writings.[26] Valkenberg writes that "it can be demonstrated that Scripture still functions as source and framework of theological *quaestiones* even where

---

22. Torrell, *Aquinas's Summa*, 5.

23. Aquinas, *ST,* Prologue.

24. Torrell, *Aquinas's Summa*, 18.

25. Davies, *Thomas Aquinas's Summa*, 147.

26. Valkenberg, "Scripture," 58.

Aquinas does not make this visible in explicit quotations."[27] Divine revelation underpins *all* that Aquinas writes.

From a slightly different angle, Denys Turner notes the highly philosophical nature of the first part of the Treatise on Human Nature. Rather than commenting on whether Aquinas sufficiently engages revelation, Turner asserts that these sorts of philosophical discussions matter to Aquinas theologically. "There is nothing in [the Treatise on Human Nature] at all that, in Thomas' view, does not have its place for good theological or pedagogical reasons."[28] Getting the philosophical positions wrong will have theological consequences.[29] While it may be impossible to know with certainty why the first part of the Treatise on Human Nature is so heavily philosophical, it is the case that a theological opinion is greatly enhanced by a strong philosophical argument, something of which Aquinas was certainly aware and makes use of.[30]

In the latter section of the Treatise on Human Nature (Q. 90–102) Aquinas works more explicitly with divine revelation. Davies writes that "these questions focus on the Genesis account of the origin of human beings and raise questions that Aquinas takes to be worth asking about that account."[31] Aquinas, like many older exegetes, understands the Genesis account literally. Indeed, he assumes the historicity of Adam and Eve. His primary interest, however, is in understanding the first couple *in relation to God*. Thus, Davies writes that Aquinas's questions here focus on the first couple, and particularly Adam, at two levels: "first, before he sinned; then after he sinned."[32] Indeed, as Torrell writes, "In perfect harmony with what revelation tells us about [man's situation in the world], Thomas Aquinas proposes a view of man and of the created universe that fully respects the

---

27. Valkenberg, "Scripture," 58.

28. Turner, "Human Person," 169.

29. Turner, "Human Person," 169. While Turner is helpful overall, I think he goes too far in suggesting that a "theological opinion is indefensible if it entails philosophical positions that are demonstrably false." I may be misunderstanding him, but it does not seem to me that every theological position is philosophically defensible. It's not clear from the opening of the *ST* that even Aquinas would agree with Turner on this point.

30. For more on how Aquinas uses this opening section of the Treatise on Human Nature to make the point that philosophy is not enough to come to knowledge of revealed truths, see Turner, "Human Person," 171–74.

31. Davies, *Thomas Aquinas's Summa*, 147.

32. Davies, *Thomas Aquinas's Summa*, 149.

reality of their autonomy and greatness."[33] This understanding offers a way into a relational anthropology set in the context of the most important relationship: that between humans and God.

Hierarchy of Created Beings

A good place to begin considering Aquinas's view of humans is with his understanding of creation as a whole. To get a sense of this, we must briefly zoom out to some of the sections of the *ST* preceding the Treatise on Human Nature. While it may seem an obvious statement to most Christians, it is important to note that at the heart of Aquinas's understanding of the world is that nothing in it exists that was not both brought into existence by God and remains in existence by its participation in God.[34] This goes along with his belief in a clear distinction between the Creator and the creature. Additionally, all creatures have a "trace" of the Trinity and are thereby related in a broad way to each other.[35]

Within creation, Aquinas categorizes all creatures into three main categories: those that are purely spiritual (angels), those that are purely corporeal (animals), and those that are both corporeal and spiritual (humans).[36] In addition, he understands all of creation—spiritual and material—in terms of a hierarchy of existence or being. To understand Aquinas's hierarchy of being is to understand how he thinks creation itself is ordered, specifically, in relation to God. DeYoung writes, "It is essential to note that all creatures have their place in the hierarchy from their relation to God, and that all things depend on God both for their coming into existence and for their continuing to exist."[37] In other words, the hierarchy assumes the Creator-creature divide and creation's dependence on God, whether you are looking at a mushroom or a human. It also takes for granted that God created all things for a purpose or "end" to which God is directing the creature. Note that the hierarchy does not include God. God is not a creature.

---

33. Torrell, *Aquinas's Summa*, 27.

34. *ST* Ia, q. 44, art. 1, co.; q. 44, art. 2, co.; q. 45, art. 2, co.

35. While much modern theology eschews "substance metaphysics" in favor of a so-called "relational ontology," it is interesting that Aquinas appears to affirm both, depending on how the latter is defined.

36. *ST* Ia, q. 50, pr.

37. DeYoung et al., *Aquinas's Ethics*, 14.

God is the Creator of all so God's relation to all created beings is as Creator, not as a part of the hierarchy of creation.

Within this hierarchy, humans fall below the angels and above other animals. Humans, therefore, are like, but not identical with, both the angels and other animals. But humans are also distinct within creation in certain ways. DeYoung et al. describe this (dis)similarity as follows: "Human beings alone possess both physical bodies and immaterial intellects [souls]; in the hierarchy we bridge the gap between material and immaterial creatures."[38] To put it another way, for Aquinas, part of what makes humans unique beings is this interesting combination of *being immaterial*, like the angels and God, yet also *being material*, like other creatures.[39] DeYoung et al. note that for Aquinas humans have the "very best sort of body and the very lowest sort of intellect."[40] Indeed, "no other intellective substance has a physical body; no other material substance has an intellect."[41] Thus, one way that humans are distinctive in creation is in their very makeup as spiritual-material beings.

In addition to this combination of material and spiritual, Aquinas is also working with a metaphysics that considers being in terms of form and matter. He thinks that all material things are composed of form and matter.[42] The distinction between form and matter involves a distinction between actuality and potentiality. Only God is infinitely actual—that is, pure act. The rest of creation is always some combination of potentiality and actuality, or becoming and being. In contrast to God who is pure act, being itself, prime matter is pure potential. Prime matter is something like a conceptual tool that exists only in the abstract, for to exist is to have form, and prime matter does not have form.[43] As Eleonore Stump writes, "Prime matter is . . . matter without any form at all, 'materiality' (as it were) apart from configuration."[44] Form is the organizing principle of matter. That is to say, form configures matter. But even if there is no matter to configure as with angels, form is necessary for existence. "For Aquinas," Stump writes,

38. DeYoung et al., *Aquinas's Ethics*, 13.

39. Aquinas, *ST* Ia, q. 75, pr.

40. DeYoung et al., *Aquinas's Ethics*, 24. See also Stump, *Aquinas*, 205.

41. DeYoung et al., *Aquinas's Ethics*, 29.

42. Stump, *Aquinas*, 194.

43. That said, it is the case that Aquinas argues that prime matter is, nonetheless, created by God. *ST* Ia, q. 44, art. 2.

44. Stump, *Aquinas*, 37.

"to be is to be configured."[45] Configuring is what forms do. "Without form," explains Stump, "nothing is actual."[46]

Souls and Capacities

This discussion of form and matter is important because it lays the foundation for another aspect of human persons that, for Aquinas, distinguishes humans from other beings: *the human soul.* It is not the mere fact that humans are ensouled beings that sets humans apart, however. Brian Davies explains that for Aquinas, "any living thing has a soul (*anima*)."[47] Aquinas thinks plants and animals are ensouled too, albeit with "vegetative" or "sensitive" souls, respectively, that are different from and inferior to human souls.[48] Indeed, Aquinas thinks that anything that is alive has a soul. He writes that the soul is "the first principle of life of those things which live: for we call living things 'animate,' and those things which have no life, 'inanimate.'"[49] What qualifies something as being alive? Aquinas writes, "Now life is shown principally by two actions, knowledge and movement."[50] Davies explains that Aquinas "thinks something alive is something able to move or operate on its own accord and not just as pushed around by something else."[51] Davies then offers this reminder to the reader of Aquinas: "When trying to understand Aquinas on soul, you need to bear in mind that his use of the word 'soul' is one that, from beginning to end, is meant

45. Stump, *Aquinas*, 37. With respect to angels, Aquinas believes angels are immaterial beings yet even as such, they are configured, or as Stump puts it, their properties are configured. Both prime matter and pure form are difficult to imagine for most of us. Even the most "unformed" matter in our imagination or experience still has form by definition. And what do configured properties look like apart from matter? All this is to say that a concrete example of prime matter is not possible, and a concrete example of form apart from matter like an angel is not generally something most of us encounter. Nonetheless, these categories are central to understanding how Aquinas describes the hierarchy of creation.

46. Stump, *Aquinas*, 37.

47. Davies, *Thomas Aquinas's Summa*, 127. It is also worth keeping in mind that *anima*, translated "soul," is the root behind the English word "animate/inanimate." This may help the reader understand what concept underlies "soul."

48. *ST* I, q. 75, art. 3, co.

49. *ST* I, q. 75, art. 1, co.

50. *ST* I, q. 75, art. 1, co.

51. Davies, *Thomas Aquinas's Summa*, 127.

to flag a distinction between things such as desks and cats—the distinction being one between 'not being alive' and 'being alive.'"[52]

So what makes the "aliveness" of humans different from that of other living beings? According to Davies, this is the main question Aquinas is addressing in *ST* Ia, Q. 75–89. Aquinas's "primary aim," writes Davies, "is to explain *what it is to be alive* as a human being, as opposed to *what it is to be alive* as, say, a cat or cabbage"[53] The difference between different living things is in the *potentiae* (capacities),[54] capacities that are associated with the type of soul that the particular creature has. Aquinas identifies five capacities of the soul: "the vegetative, the sensitive, the appetitive, the locomotion, and the intellective."[55] Davies offers a helpful description of the first four of these capacities:

> Something has vegetative powers . . . if it is able to feed or nourish itself, if it is able to grow, and if it is able to reproduce (Ia,78,2). Sensitive powers . . . lead things to be able to latch onto the world by touch, sight, taste, hearing, or smell (Ia,78,3). Something with an appetite is an individual that is naturally drawn to goods of various kinds that it senses, while something capable of locomotion is just able to move around under its own steam (as it were).[56]

Humans share these capacities with other living beings within the hierarchy.

In contrast to other living beings, however, the human soul is both subsistent and has intellective capacity.[57] To say the soul is subsistent is simply to say that it can "have an operation 'per se' apart from the body."[58] To describe the soul as having "intellective" capacity is to say that humans

---

52. Davies, *Thomas Aquinas's Summa*, 128. Note also that when speaking of humans Aquinas interchanges the word "soul" with "intellect" and sometimes "intellective soul" or, less frequently in the *ST*, "mind." In this essay, I will generally refer to the human soul as exactly that: human soul. When I discuss Aquinas's understanding of the unique capacity of the human soul—the intellect—I will use either "intellect" or "intellective" as a modifier of capacity. So, to say "human soul" is identical to saying intellective or rational soul, terms that signal that the soul we are discussing is a *human* soul, not some other sort of soul.

53. Davies, *Thomas Aquina's Summa*, 128, emphasis in original.

54. Davies suggests several translations here: "abilities," "powers," or "capacities." Because "capacities" is often used in reference to Aquinas's understanding of the soul that is the word I will use.

55. *ST* I, q. 78, s.c.

56. Davies, *Thomas Aquinas's Summa*, 127.

57. *ST* I, q. 78, art. 1, co; *ST* I, q. 75, art. 2.

58. *ST* I, q. 75, art. 2, co.

have a capacity that goes beyond merely being alive. Aquinas writes, "the soul is the primary principle of our nourishment, sensation, and local movement; and likewise of our understanding. Therefore, this principle by which we primarily understand, whether it be called the intellect or the intellectual soul, is the form of the body."[59] When Aquinas states that the intellective capacity is the principle by which we understand, he is pointing to an important difference between humans and other creatures. As Davies humorously writes, "One might truly think of a cat as having vegetative, sensitive, appetitive, and locomotive abilities, but cats cannot give you a lecture on what cats are; they are not things with understanding express-ible linguistically."[60] Understood in terms of capacities, cats do not have the intellective capacity for doing so. Humans, by contrast, do have the capacity to know and understand.

It is important to recognize, however, that what Aquinas has in mind with "capacity" is not a physical capacity for understanding, but a *metaphysical* capacity, that is, a metaphysical *potentiality* for understand-ing. This intellective potentiality, like other potentialities, may not be fully actualized. Nonetheless, it is the case that all humans are endowed with this potential for knowing and understanding that, as DeYoung et al. write, "allow[s] them to engage with the creation in a way that mirrors the Creator more closely than other creatures."[61] It is this intellective capacity of the soul that distinguishes humans from other living beings.

One additional difference between human and animal souls is that human souls are, as Aquinas puts it, "not said to be produced, like the life of other animals, by air or water, but immediately by God."[62] The soul as the form of the body, in other words, is created by God as the soul of some particular body, organizing the matter of that particular body. Take, for example, my soul. My soul is not some generic soul that preexisted my body and then entered my body at some particular point in time, animating it and giving it life. No, my soul is created by God to organize matter into my particular body. In other words, Aquinas understands the intellective soul to be the organizing principle of the matter that is some particular person's body.[63] What this means, according to DeYoung et al., is that the intellec-

---

59. *ST* I, q. 76, art. 1, co.; q. 76, art. 4, s.c.

60. Davies, *Thomas Aquinas's Summa*, 127.

61. DeYoung et al, *Aquinas's Ethics*, 22.

62. *ST* I, q. 72, ad 1.

63. Aquinas, *ST* I, q. 76, art. 1, s.c.; q. 76, art. 4, s.c., co. One can refer to the soul as

tive soul "organizes and structures matter into a living, organic human substance with species-specific biological processes and functions."[64] Even more precisely, the human soul organizes matter not just into a particular species, but into some *specific human person.*

The importance of understanding the soul as the form of the body in no way undermines the importance of the body for Aquinas, nor does it in any way give preference to the soul over the body. While we may say that I *have* a soul, this language is a bit misleading from Aquinas's perspective. Plato's dualistic model of humans, where the soul *is* the person and the body does not seem all that necessary, is rejected by Aquinas. Indeed, after considering two ways in which perhaps the soul could be considered the "man" and noting his disagreement with Plato, Aquinas writes that "it is clear that man is not a soul only, but something composed of body and soul."[65] The soul by itself, for Aquinas, is in some way incomplete. Denys Turner writes that Aquinas prefers Aristotle's version of human persons over Plato's just because Aristotle's version "yields the theologically right conclusion: nothing that shows the bare survival of my soul is sufficient to show my survival as a person."[66] The person as "soul" is not fully a person. Similarly, the body is not some sort of add-on that can be disposed of. A person's soul extends to the entire body of that person, "in each part thereof."[67] Additionally, the capacities of the soul cannot be fully actualized apart from the body. DeYoung et al. point out that "on Aquinas's account of human nature, embodiment is a great good, a state not to be endured or bemoaned, but rather embraced."[68] Just as the soul by itself is not a human, so the body by itself is not a human.

In modern debates about the soul, Aquinas's rendering of humans as a body-soul complex fits well with what John Cooper describes as "holism." Holism is the idea that "human life involves an operational part-whole

---

organizing matter or the form of matter. For the sake of consistency and clarity, I will refer to it as organizing matter rather than the form of matter. The substantial form is the organizing principle of the matter involved.

64. DeYoung et al., *Aquinas's Ethics*, 34.

65. *ST* I, q. 76, art. 4, co.

66. Turner, "Human Person," 172.

67. Aquinas, *ST* I, q. 76, art. 8, co. See also *Summa Contra Gentiles* 2, q. 72. According to Norman Kretzmann, this is also affirmed in *De Anima*, 10c. See Kretzmann, *Metaphysics of Creation*, 332–33.

68. DeYoung et al., *Aquinas's Ethics*, 31. See also Aquinas, *ST* I, q. 89, art. 1, s.c.

relation."[69] In other words, *the body-soul complex together is the person.* The body-soul complex is something like a fresh-baked loaf of yeast bread. The yeast is an integral aspect of the bread. In *some* sense, one could say it is the "form" of the bread.[70] The material of even the simplest loaf—flour, water, salt, and butter or oil—will not become bread without the yeast. The yeast penetrates all parts of the dough, taking in sugar and giving off carbon dioxide, bringing the dough life and forming it into a loaf of bread that can then be baked. The "matter" of flour, water, salt, and fat are merely *potential* bread without the yeast. Likewise, the yeast, set aside by the baker for the particular loaf it will enliven, needs the "matter" that makes up the dough to form into bread. Although this is not a perfect analogy, at least in part because yeast itself is matter while the soul is not, it does offer a picture of how the body and soul are intended to operate together something like the dough and the yeast. The soul, like the yeast, is integrated into all parts of the body enlivening and animating it. The bread is the sort of bread it is (yeast bread) because the dough is suitable for the addition of yeast in order for it to grow and develop into just the type of loaf the baker intended. In a similar way, the human body is the sort of body that it is because it is fitting for rational ensoulment. Of course there is a dis-analogy here as well: while the yeast is basically useless without (other) matter to work with, the soul, on Aquinas's account, does have some ability to operate apart from the body.

For Aquinas, the soul not only can exist without the body, but in fact when a person dies it does exist apart from the body, albeit in a diminished state.[71] This diminished state is primarily due to the fact that after death a body is no longer present to take in various sorts of sensory information like color or hunger or pain. Disembodied survival is not natural for humans. Turner explains that humans are "environmentally dependent in multiple ways, not just for bodily food, but also for food for thought." He goes on, "Otherwise than as thus embodied, the only understanding they can have of anything by means of their natural powers is, [Aquinas] says . . .

69. Cooper, "Scripture and Philosophy," 32.

70. However, I must stress that this is only an analogy, and I am not suggesting that the yeast is literally the form of the bread, in the sense Aristotle and Aquinas use the word "form." The yeast is, in fact, one of the *material* causes of the bread, not its *formal* cause. Analogies cannot do everything. What this simple analogy is seeking to emphasize is the *complete unity* of body and soul in human beings.

71. *ST* I, q. 89, s.c.

'general' and 'undifferentiated' (*in quadam communitate et confusione*)."[72] In other words, although the soul survives death, the disembodied soul is very limited in what it is able to do. Nonetheless, as Stump puts it, "although a person is not identical to his soul, the existence of the soul is sufficient for the existence of the person."[73]

Aquinas's account of the composition of humans is helpful because it resists reductionistic impulses that would suggest the person merely consists of the actions performed by her soul or that she is nothing more than the actions performed by her body. Rather, he recognizes the complexity of this composite being whose systems cannot easily be reduced to the operation of some particular entity or part of that system.[74] He writes, "Body and soul are not two actually existing substances; rather, the two of them together constitute one actually existing substance."[75] As DeYoung et al. explain, "On Aquinas's account, the human being is a completely unified, individual substance, composed of matter and form, and *not* one substance somehow composed of two further substances."[76] As we will soon see, however, this conception is not without problems.

Disembodied Intellective Souls

There is a tension in Aquinas's thinking about how to understand what the human soul is, and how it is that the soul can survive death. Stump points out one of those problems. At death, in Stump's words, the soul as form becomes a configurer with nothing to configure.[77] This seems like a problem.[78] But even apart from this tension within his thinking, a tension

72. Turner, "Human Person," 172.

73. Stump, *Aquinas*, 53.

74. Very simply put, the whole is more than the sum of its parts. For a more complete explanation of this see Stump, *Aquinas*, 197. See also *ST* I, q. 76, art. 2, co. where Aquinas argues that humans do not have multiple souls but only one soul with multiple powers and that, therefore, humans are "absolutely one."

75. Aquinas, *SCG* 2, q. 69.

76. DeYoung et al., *Aquinas's Ethics*, 33.

77. Stump, *Aquinas*, 204. Because much of Stump's explanation comes from sources other than the *ST*, I am for this book's limited scope relying on her very capable description of how Aquinas responds to this problem.

78. Specifically the tension has to do with Aquinas's use of Aristotle and the view of some that Aquinas's thought regarding the soul's persistence after death is incoherent. See, for example, Kevin Corcoran, *Rethinking Human Nature*, 37–40. Many Thomist

for modern readers the bigger problem is whether the intellective capacity can exist and function apart from matter, that is, apart from a material brain. Perhaps more to the point, is there such a thing as an immaterial subsistent intellect? Some might say no, but for theists, as Stump points out, such a thing as an immaterial intellect must be possible. As she argues, "An argument for the impossibility of an immaterial mind [intellect] would be in effect an argument against the existence of God, and so far no one has produced such an argument that has garnered any substantial support."[79] Indeed, God is spirit, according to Scripture, and clearly intellective given the actions described in Scripture. Thus Stump's argument appears correct regardless of whether or not one wants to actually affirm an immaterial intellective capacity for humans.

So what does Aquinas think the subsistent human soul can do apart from the body? Perhaps it is easiest to understand what the human soul can do apart from a body by first discussing the necessity of the body for much of what the human soul does. Throughout his discussion of the soul, Aquinas refers to the capacities or powers of the soul. As briefly noted earlier, for Aquinas, these capacities should not be thought of as physical capabilities but as human potentialities. Humans have numerous capacities in the soul that are able to be actualized in the body-soul composite. As DeYoung et al. write, "The rational [intellective] soul is what accounts for all the things the body can do."[80] For various reasons, however, not all of these capacities will be able to be fully actualized. Take sight, for example. A person who is nearsighted is able to see, but she cannot see things at a distance well. The soul's capacity for sight is actualized through her eyes, but not perfectly because of the misshapen lenses in her eyes.[81] If the person becomes blind,

---

scholars, however, do not think this tension is unresolvable. See, for example, Anthony Freeman's brief explanation of how Aquinas's compromise enhanced Christian theology, "Editorial Introduction," in *Modern Believing* 57.2 (2016). For more complete treatments see also Eleonore Stump, *Aquinas*, 204–10; Gilson, *The Christian Philosophy of St. Thomas Aquinas*, 197–99; Davies, *The Thought of Thomas Aquinas*, 215–16, and *Thomas Aquinas's Summa Theologiae: A Guide and Commentary*, 126–34. For more background on Aquinas's own understanding of the soul apart from his work in the ST, see Bazán, "The Human Soul: Form and Substance?"

79. Stump, *Aquinas*, 204. For Aquinas, this argument holds for the angels too since they, like God and unlike humans, are spiritual intellective beings.

80. DeYoung et al., *Aquinas's Ethics*, 52.

81. Specifically, this impacts the sensitive appetite of the soul. The distinctions between the appetites or powers of the soul are interesting but the constraints of length do not allow me to discuss them here. See also DeYoung et al., *Aquinas's Ethics*, 65; Stump, *Aquinas*, 54.

the capacity for sight will no longer be actualized at all. To paraphrase Jesus, the soul is willing but the flesh is weak.

While this distinction between potential and actual may seem abstract at first glance because the discussion surrounds something invisible—the soul—it is not hard to come up with similar physical examples. To continue with the example of sight, we can recognize something like this distinction between potential and actual with respect to the physical structures involved in sight. A person can have a fully functioning optic nerve, for example, with all the necessary connections needed for sight. But if for some reason the person's eyes are badly damaged—say, by an accident or due to something in their prenatal development—she will not be able to actualize that potential, even if her optic nerve remains intact.[82] It is important to keep in mind that while the inability to fully actualize a capacity of the soul through the body may hamper some variety of happiness in this life, the lack of physical actualization of a capacity in no way renders the person anything less than fully human nor hinders their potential for beatitude in the life to come.

The intellective capacities of the soul, however, operate differently than capacities associated with other powers of the soul.[83] For Aquinas, the intellective capacity rises above the other capacities. "Although the operation of the intellect has its origin in the senses: yet, in the thing apprehended through the senses, the intellect knows many things which the senses cannot perceive."[84] Humans, because of their intellective capacity, are able to go beyond mere information and contemplate what the senses have presented to them, knowing things about the object that are not immediately apparent to the senses. In short, humans are "able to think," writes Davies, "able to proceed from sensation to reflection and argument."[85] This ability, for Aquinas, lies in the operation of the intellective capacity of the soul.[86] The key difference between the human soul and the soul of other sorts of animals (and other lower creatures) is our ability for both *knowing* and *understanding*. It is our ability to receive the form of something, to know not

---

82. That the optic nerve can retain its potential is demonstrated by doctors who are able to stimulate the optic nerve of blind people whose eyes are damaged, allowing them to "see" light.

83. Vegetative, sensitive, appetitive, locomotive. *ST* I, q. 78, art. 1, s.c.

84. Aquinas, *ST* I, q. 78, art. 8, ad. 4.

85. Davies, *Thomas Aquinas's Summa*, 136.

86. Aquinas, *ST* I, q. 78, art. 1, co.

just *that* it is, but *what* it is in itself by nature, the "whatness" of the thing, what it is for the thing to be. It is more than simply knowing that a thing is this and not that or that a thing exists. It is understanding the *nature* of the thing. Or maybe we could say that to understand something is to know *why* it is this and not that; the ability to contemplate what it is that makes something what it is.

In its existence apart from the body, the soul is seriously curtailed in its ability to actualize its capacities. Without a body the soul cannot process sensory information because there are no senses to take in information just as there is no body to take in food. The capacity that *is* able to be actualized without the body, however, is the capacity for understanding.[87] Aquinas writes that the "soul can understand when it is apart from the body."[88] This is because while the physical organ assists and supports the intellect in cognition while embodied, the physical organ itself does not perform cognition, the intellective soul does.

DeYoung et al. offer an excellent explanation of how cognition works apart from the body:

> Although Aquinas claims that the body is intimately involved in the process of human cognition, he draws a careful distinction between what is necessary to *support* an activity and what is required to *perform* the activity. Unlike nutrition and sensation, which require the body for carrying out their proper activities, the intellect does not require matter for the actual act of cognition. The act of nutrition requires there to be a body to digest food, and the act of perception requires that there be a body to smell the coffee, but, on Aquinas's account, intellective cognition is an "organless" activity. The human *brain* is not what thinks—the immaterial *intellect* is. Or, more properly speaking, the human being thinks by means of her intellect.[89]

The intellective capacity of the soul is what *knows* or *thinks* about things. The corporeal organ, the brain, supports this thinking, but the thinking is done by the intellective soul itself.

Aquinas makes clear that although the soul can be separated from the body and still function to some degree, this is not its natural state. He writes, "It is united to the body in order that it may have an existence and

---

87. Aquinas, *ST* I, q. 77, art. 8, s.c., co.

88. Aquinas, *ST* I, q. 89, art. 1, s.c.

89. DeYoung et al., *Aquinas's Ethics*, 41.

an operation suitable to its nature."[90] As the lowest form of intellective substances, the human soul relies on the body in certain ways that other intellective substances like the angels do not. The nature of the human soul is to be joined to a body. "Nevertheless," writes Aquinas, "it is possible for it to exist apart from the body and also to understand in another way."[91] What is this "other way" to understand that Aquinas is suggesting? Just as the human soul needs support from the body in this life, in its temporarily disembodied state the soul receives support from "superior things" through the "light of grace."[92] Specifically, the human soul is supported by God.

The importance of the intellective capacities of the soul to continue to exist in a disembodied state cannot be underestimated. In Aquinas's model, the capacities for knowing and loving, those that are most easily identified with being human, are not negated by the lack of a material body. More than that, the capacity to know and love God is the proper "end" or *telos* of humans. In other words, to reach one's ultimate end or purpose of knowing and loving God perfectly, something not attainable in this life, relies on the ability of the person to survive death. Only after death will we know as we are known (1 Cor 13:12). Although the human capacities are deficient without a body, the intellective capacity of the soul can continue to function in a "residual form," as Turner puts it.[93]

Although disembodied souls will experience this foretaste of eternal bliss after death, this should not be understood as the *final* state. For Aquinas, as for the Christian tradition as a whole, our full salvation awaits the resurrection of the dead on the last day. At that time, the disembodied souls, which cannot fully operate apart from their bodies, will be rejoined with their bodies on a restored and renewed earth to be with the Lord forever. In the city of God, those who have served Christ will "see his face and his name will be on their foreheads." Together, "they will reign for ever and ever" (Rev 21:4, 5).

Image of God

In the historic Christian tradition, perhaps the most important feature of humans that distinguishes them from other animals is the image of God.

90. Aquinas, *ST* I, q. 89, art. 1, co.
91. Aquinas, *ST* I, q. 89, art. 1, co.
92. Aquinas, *ST* I, q. 89, art. 1, ad 3.
93. Turner, "Human Person," 172.

For Aquinas, humans are not just subsistent beings consisting of matter and form; we are created *in the image of God*.[94] Working with Genesis 1:26, Aquinas, like many premodern exegetes, makes a distinction between image and likeness. Quoting Augustine, he writes, "Where an image exists, there forthwith is a likeness; but where there is likeness, there is not necessarily an image."[95] For Aquinas, "image" indicates something that is "produced as an imitation of something else," in this case, God, whereas a "likeness" merely resembles something but is not copied from it. Aquinas uses the illustration of an egg here to help make his point. "An egg," he writes, "however much like and equal to another egg, is not called an image of the other egg, because it is not copied from it."[96] An image, therefore, "adds something to likeness."[97]

Nonetheless, even an image is not identical to the exemplar from which it was copied. Aquinas makes clear that an exemplar always surpasses its copy, yet the copy resembles the exemplar quite well (although not perfectly). Davies explains that "something can be *like* another thing because it resembles it in *some* way. But an *image* of something resembles it fairly *precisely*, and, thinks Aquinas, human beings resemble God in quite precise ways even though they are as creatures unequal to God, and are therefore imperfect images of God."[98] The point is that humans are not perfect images of God. Only Christ, who is of the same essence as the Father, is the perfect image of God.

Aquinas associates the image of God with the soul. He states that the image of God is "impressed" on or belongs to the human soul only, a statement that clearly sets humans apart from "beasts" because animals do not possess an intellective soul. He writes, "Man's excellence consists in the fact that God made him to His own image by giving him an intellectual soul, which raises him above the beasts of the field."[99] In other words, to speak of humans as the image of God is to speak of beings who possess a intellective soul that, according to Aquinas, "has a capacity for the highest good."[100] What is this highest good? It is what Aquinas calls a "natural aptitude for

---

94. Aquinas, *ST* I, q. 93, art. 1, s.c.
95. Aquinas, *ST* I, q. 93, art. 1, co.
96. Aquinas, *ST* I, q. 93, art. 1, co.
97. Aquinas, *ST* I, q. 93, art. 1, co.
98. Davies, *Thomas Aquinas's Summa*, 148.
99. Aquinas, *ST* I, q. 93, art. 2, s.c.
100. Aquinas, *ST* I, q. 93, ad 3.

understanding and loving God."[101] This aptitude is at the center of what it means that humans are like God.

Aquinas thinks that God is an intellective being who knows and loves himself. According to DeYoung et al., Aquinas believes that "the creatures capable of engaging with the world *most* fully are intellective beings, since intellective creatures can know and love the beings around them in ways similar, in relevant respects, to God's knowledge and love."[102] To put this in more contemporary terms, Aquinas is arguing that all humans have a natural capacity for relationship, most especially relationship with their Creator. This capacity for relationship resides in the intellective capacities of the soul. The human capacity to love others, to be in interpersonal relationships, is like God's own relational self. Human imitation of God is not perfect but nonetheless is seen in three ways. Aquinas writes:

> First, inasmuch as man possesses a natural aptitude for understanding and loving God; and this aptitude consists in the very nature of the mind, which is common to all men. Secondly, inasmuch as man actually and habitually knows and loves God, though imperfectly; and this image consists in the conformity of grace. Thirdly, inasmuch as man knows and loves God perfectly; and this image consists in the likeness of glory.[103]

Clearly for Aquinas, all people are made in the image of God with the capacity to know and love God. Like all capacities, however, this capacity must be actualized. Life is characterized by movement either toward God or away from God. For those who are in Christ, the actualization of the relational capacity to know and love God throughout our lives by grace moves us toward our ultimate end: beatitude.[104] In other words, the capacity for relationship put forward by Aquinas is a deep-seated, grace-assisted teleological capacity.

---

101. Aquinas, *ST* I, q. 93, art. 4, s.c.

102. DeYoung et al., *Aquinas's Ethics*, 17.

103. Aquinas, *ST* I, q. 93, art. 4, co.

104. Although Aquinas does not deal with the human capacity to know and love others in this section of the *ST*, it is reasonable to suggest that knowing and loving others would be an outgrowth of this capacity to know and love God as the two great commandments suggest. Thanks to Casey Jen for this question.

Conclusion

I have described in this chapter Aquinas's anthropology as presented in the Treatise on Human Nature. I will now briefly review some of the most important features of his view. As intellective beings, only humans are able to organize their lives willfully in accordance with their end, thereby attaining perfect happiness or beatitude in the final state. Non-intellective beings, in Aquinas's scheme, cannot reach beatitude because they do not have the requisite capacities to do so.[105] More precisely, they do not have an intellective soul. As DeYoung et al. put it, "No matter how many of its capacities it actualizes, an iguana can never reach beatitude,"[106] although it can attain its intended *telos*. Only intellective beings can reach beatitude—that is, can know and love God.

When the various aspects of Aquinas's account of humans are put together, we get a finely detailed picture of humanity. By modern standards, it may appear that Aquinas has left certain important topics out, like gender and race.[107] But of course those are not the issues of his time. One could say, however, that Aquinas's depiction of humanity encompasses even topics like those, without explicitly addressing them. This is because Aquinas's account is not exclusive to just some sorts of humans. Rather, his model takes account of *all* beings born from human parents, as well as the first created humans, Adam and Eve. Additionally, all humans are considered not just as abstract substances, but as complex persons, with a created structure that enables them to function comprehensively in relationship with God, whereby they are not just known and loved by God but know and love him in return.

Keeping Aquinas's overall framework of humans and their place in the created order in mind, the next chapter will turn to the biblical texts. By examining seminal texts like Genesis 1 and 2, as well as various depictions of humans throughout the Old and New Testaments, chapter 2 will consider whether and how humans might be thought of as unique from a biblical perspective.

---

105. Aquinas, *ST* I-II, q. 1, art. 8, co.

106. DeYoung et al., *Aquinas's Ethics*, 51.

107. It is worth noting, however, that Aquinas does affirm that women are the image of God. *ST* I, q. 93, art. 4, ad.1.

2

Biblical Anthropology

IN THE LAST CHAPTER we explored Aquinas as an example of a theologian who, using Scripture, tradition, and the tools of reason, worked out a detailed understanding of human persons as unique beings within the created order. For Aquinas, humans are beings that are both like and unlike other created beings, as well as like and unlike God. In their possession of a rational soul, humans are like the angels and God. But unlike God and the angels, humans have a physical body. In other words, humans are a unity of body and rational soul. It is especially the rational soul that, for Aquinas, is associated with the image of God and gives humans their unique dignity and place within the visible created order.

In this chapter I will look more closely at Scripture and its overall portrayal of human persons. I will begin by examining the first two chapters of Genesis. This examination will show that the story of God's creation of the first humans in these chapters distinguishes them from the rest of creation. I will then examine the image of God as described in Scripture in the context of the ancient Near East. I will conclude this section by surveying Scripture as a whole to demonstrate how human uniqueness is portrayed in the broad story of creation, fall, redemption, and consummation.

Beginnings in Genesis

The book of Genesis is about beginnings. It tells about the beginning of God's creative acts, the beginning of various forms of life, the beginning

33

of humans, and the beginning of God separating out a people for himself in order to bless the world. This book of beginnings is typically divided into two main segments. Genesis 1–11 is considered the primeval history, and Genesis 12–50 is the patriarchal history.[1] Within this larger twofold structure is the tenfold structure formed by the *toledot*, or generations.[2]

Julius Wellhausen, the father of the Documentary Hypothesis, and his successors found even more potential divisions within the narrative structure. These divisions were based on hypothetical sources initially labeled as J, E, D, and P, although over time more were added. More recently, scholarship has turned toward a more literary-historical-grammatical reading of the text, less concerned with who may have authored the various parts of the text and more interested in the final form of the text as the community of believers—Jewish or Christian—has received it.[3] This focus on the final form of the text as it has been received will be the method employed in this chapter.[4]

Genesis 1–2

Genesis 1–11, the primeval history, includes six of the ten *toledot* divisions in the book of Genesis as a whole. Genesis 1–2 includes the introductory

---

1. Most commentaries dealing with Genesis assume this division. For a few examples, see Speiser, *Genesis*, liii; Alter, *Genesis*, xliii; Wenham, *Genesis 1–15*, xxii; Westermann, *Genesis 1–11*, 2.

2. The *toledots* are as follows: 2:4—4:26, history of heaven and earth; 5:1—6:8, family history of Adam; 6:9—9:29, family history of Noah; 10:1—11:9, family history of Noah's sons; 11:10–26, family history of Shem; 11:27—25:11, family history of Terah; 25:12–18, family history of Ishmael; 25:19—35:29, family history of Isaac; 36:1—37:1, family history of Esau; 37:2—50:26, family history of Jacob. Taken from Wenham, *Genesis 1–15*, xxii.

3. For more on the Documentary Hypothesis, see Whybray, *Making of the Pentateuch*; Bergman, *Inconsistency in the Torah*.

4. While the Documentary Hypothesis and its various permutations can aid one in discerning various linguistic patterns and themes within the larger narrative, a close literary reading achieves the same end without the inevitable fragmentation that occurs with a dependence on JEDP. In addition, as a Christian reader of the text who affirms the doctrine of inspiration, I recognize the primary author as God and thus understand the text as it has come to the church as a cohesive whole, intended to tell one story—the story of salvation. For other reasons not based on the doctrine of inspiration to affirm working with the final form of the text, see Alter, *Genesis*, xl–xlii; also Fox, *The Five Books of Moses*, xx–xxi.

chapter or prologue, Genesis 1:1—2:3,[5] as well as the first part of the first *toledot,* the account or generations of the heavens and the earth, which consists of Genesis 2:4—4:26.

It is difficult not to notice that the first two chapters of Genesis appear to tell two different creation stories. Older scholarship tended to emphasize these differences by citing distinct authors and reading these two chapters as separate accounts.[6] More recently, however, scholars recognize that Genesis 1 and 2 form a coherent whole that should be held together. Terence Fretheim, for example, suggests just such a coherent reading, noting that P, the supposed source of the first account, was most likely the redactor of the second account.[7] Because of this, "a theologically coherent perspective on creation, which the P writer presumably had, is to be found in the two chapters *in interaction with each other.*"[8] In other words, Fretheim argues that reading these two chapters as a single unit is necessary for proper understanding and interpretation.[9] With that in mind, then, I will begin with a close examination of Genesis 1:1—2:3, followed by Genesis 2:3–25, understanding one account in the light of the other.

The Orderly Creation

The importance of order can be found throughout the Pentateuch. The creation account in Genesis 1 provides the backdrop to this preoccupation with order. Here God is presented as the God who brings order out of chaos, who orders the universe to allow life to flourish and make it habitable for human persons. The goodness of creation is related to the orderliness of creation. In a similar way, sin is related to disorder or the disruption of the orderliness of creation.

Genesis 1 opens with these familiar words: "In the beginning God created the heavens and the earth. Now the earth was formless and empty,

5. Genesis 1:1—2:3 has been argued in Old Testament studies to be a prologue or introduction to the book. For example, see Walton, *Genesis 1 as Ancient Cosmology,* 124–27.

6. For a modern example of this pattern, see James Brownson's account of Genesis 2 in *Bible, Gender, and Sexuality,* 86–90. Brownson treats Genesis 2 apart from and without reference to Genesis 1.

7. Fretheim, *God and the World,* 33.

8. Fretheim, *God and the World,* 33, emphasis original.

9. Others who argue for a cohesive reading of Genesis 1–2 include, for example, Brueggemann, *Genesis,* 14–15, 40; Reno, *Genesis,* 81–83.

darkness was over the surface of the deep, and the Spirit of God was hovering over the waters" (Gen 1:1–2). Although some have argued that this account should be understood as a scientific recounting of the beginning of the earth,[10] others recognize that modern imposition of scientific categories on this ancient document leads one to miss the central focus of the text.[11] Commentator Gordon Wenham suggests that the central focus of Genesis 1:1—2:3, in contrast to other creation accounts in the ancient Near East, is to affirm YHWH as the all-powerful Creator, and humans and the rest of creation as creatures.[12] In other words, central to this story is a clear distinction between the Creator and the creation, a distinction that is also central to understanding humans and their place in creation.

Like many other ancient Near Eastern creation accounts, Genesis 1 includes notions of some sort of primordial chaos.[13] Susan Niditch writes, "The period of chaos in Genesis 1 is described by the rhyming terms *tohu* (formless) and *bohu* (void), by the image of darkness on the face of the deep, and by the presence of the spirit of the Lord hovering over the face of the water."[14] This "formless void" is not conducive to life, human or other life. Only after God begins to order the chaos, are living beings added to the picture. Walter Brueggemann suggests that chaos is a force that "seeks to negate and nullify the world as a secure place of blessing."[15] From this perspective, chaos—alternately named Rahab, Tannim, Leviathan, Behemoth, Yam, or Nahar—is opposed to God.[16] Another perspective, like

---

10. Morris, *Remarkable Birth*, iv.

11. See, for example, Collins, *Reading Genesis Well*; Waltke, "Literary Genre," 2–10; Andersen, *From Creation to New Creation*, 1; Nürnberger, "Conquest of Chaos," 45; Young, "Christianity and the Age of the Earth," 83–94; and Jaki, *Genesis 1 through the Ages*, to name a few.

12. Wenham, *Genesis 1–15*, 5.

13. The idea of chaos is well known in various ancient Near Eastern creation accounts. As noted further on, commentators disagree on precisely how to understand this idea in the Genesis account. Whatever else one says about it, chaos is not understood as evil or a personal agent here. Rather, it has to do with an incompleteness, a not-yet-orderedness, as especially implied in Gen 1:2, where the earth is described as a "formless void." Only after God begins to order the chaos are living beings added to the picture.

14. Niditch, *Chaos to Cosmos*, 18. For a further discussion of *tohu* and *bohu*, see Walton, *Genesis 1 as Ancient Cosmology*, 140–44.

15. Brueggemann, *Theology of the Old Testament*, 533.

16. Gunkel, "Influence of Babylonian Mythology," 25–52. In this classic essay Gunkel offers instances throughout the Old Testament where chaos is referred to with these terms. See especially pp. 35–40.

that of Michael Deroche, suggests that the chaos of Genesis 1 "is an inert mass lacking order or differentiation."[17] Likewise, according to Terence Fretheim, "The chaos of [Gen 1:2] refers not to some divine opponent (unlike Babylonian parallels), or even a force, but to raw material that God uses to create what follows, when it [the chaos] ceases to exist."[18] Regardless of how one settles the issue of chaos, Genesis 1 describes God creating by his word, ordering the formless, incomplete beginning of Genesis 1:1 into a place of life.

The method of God's ordering in Genesis 1 is via separation and division. The Hebrew word *bdl* is a key word in this text. In fact, the largest clustering of *bdl* occurs in this chapter where it is used five times.[19] According to the Brown-Driver-Briggs lexicon, *bdl* means "to be divided, separate."[20] The basic idea is separation.[21] God's ordering of the world through separations (*bdl*) yields a "good" (*tov*) creation. Examples of *bdl* outside of Genesis 1 include separating the priests from the people for service in Numbers 8:16, as well as separating things into clean and unclean, and separating Israel from the nations in Leviticus.

In Genesis 1, God brings order out of the primeval disorder by separating various elements thereby establishing boundaries between them. Light is separated from darkness (v. 4), the waters above are separated from the waters below (vv. 6–7), and the lights in the sky separate day from night (vv. 14, 18). Water and dry land, light and darkness do not belong together. To blur or erase the boundaries between these elements is to destroy their individual identifying characteristics. Throughout the creation account, *bdl* is used to emphasize "that the creator-God is a God of order rather than a mythological procreator."[22] Gordon Wenham states that "separation is one of the central ideas in this chapter."[23] Deroche concurs, noting that "the acts of separation are those most fundamental to the Genesis notion of creation."[24] Without these basic distinctions (or separations) of light and darkness, day and night, and water above from water below, life—especially

---

17. Deroche, "Isaiah XLV 7 and the Creation of Chaos," 11.

18. Fretheim, *Pentateuch*, 73.

19. Gen 1:4, 6, 7, 14, 18.

20. Brown, Driver, and Briggs, *Hebrew and English Lexicon*, s.v. "*bdl*."

21. Van Dam, "*bdl*."

22. Otzen, "*bdl*."

23. Wenham, *Genesis 1–15*, 18.

24. Deroche, "Isaiah XLV 7 and the Creation of Chaos," 15.

human life—could not exist. Milgrom notes that "separation creates order, and the distinctions between the elements must be maintained lest the world collapse into chaos and confusion."[25] It is no surprise, therefore, that all of these separations occur and such boundaries are established before any life is created.

Adding to the picture of order and separation presented in Genesis 1 is the description of things being created "according to their kind." The plants produce seeds "according to their kind" (v. 11). Living creatures are created "according to their kind" (v. 21). Vegetation and creatures, like the elements of the earth, stay within their created boundaries, reproducing not in a haphazard, mixed-up way, but according to their kind. The ordered environment with water separated from dry land, plants bearing seed according to their kinds, the great lights of the sky separating night and day, living creatures of the sky and sea created according to their kind, and animals on the land created according to their kind are all declared by God to be *good* (vv. 10, 18, 21, 25).

Verse 26 moves to the creation of the first humans. Interestingly, the key word *bdl* does not occur with the creation of humans. Humans do not appear to be created by separation of one thing from another. Nor are they said to be created "according to their kind." Phyllis Trible points out that the difference in vocabulary between the creation of humans and the rest of creation signals their unique nature.[26] So far, the story has described creation in terms like, "let the land," or "let the water," or "let there be." But with the creation of the humans, the story shifts in several ways.

First, only the creation of humans depicts God's self-deliberation concerning what the purpose of this creation will be (v. 26):

> Let us make *adam* in our image, according to our likeness,
> so that they may rule over the fish of the sea[27]
> and the birds of the air
> and the cattle and all the earth

25. Milgrom, *Leviticus 17–22*, 1761.

26. Trible, *God and the Rhetoric of Sexuality*, 15.

27. Some earlier translations, including the 1985 NIV, ignore or mistranslate this clause as "and let them rule." However, the verbal sequence here of a cohortative ("Let us make . . .") followed by an imperfect (". . . they will rule") is best translated as a purpose clause ("*so that* they may rule"). Most current English translations reflect this important understanding. See Lambdin, *Introduction to Biblical Hebrew*, 119. For further confirmation of this translation, see also Middleton, *Liberating Image*, 53.

and everything that creeps upon the earth. (translation mine)

Creation has been moving along through the days up to this point, each day bringing something new into being. Now, in the middle of the sixth day, there seems to be a pause. As with every other creation, God has declared the animals good. Here, however, instead of the expected "and it was evening and morning, the sixth day," God says to himself "let us make." This little interlude itself sets humans apart as distinct, as unique from the rest of creation.

The second way that humans are distinguished from the rest of creation in this text is that only humans are created for a specific, named purpose. Humans, unlike the rest of creation, are created by God for a purpose disclosed to the reader in God's self-deliberation. Humans will be created "so that they may rule." They have a God-given vocation: they will be God's representative rulers over the created order. Their purpose, sewn into their very existence, is to rule the newly created earth, maintaining God's orderly arrangement.[28]

The third distinctive feature of the humans, one connected to their purpose, is God's direct address to them. After the creation of humans, God personally addresses them (vv. 28–29) first with a blessing, and then with a speech that grants them the gift of food. God blesses the fish and birds using similar language (v. 22) to that by which he blesses the humans, but only the humans are given the further charge to subdue (*kabash*) and have dominion (*radah*).

> And God blessed them,
> and God said unto them,
> "Be fruitful, and become numerous, and fill the earth, and subdue it:
> and have dominion over the fish of the sea,
> and over the birds of the air,
> and over every living creature that creeps upon the earth."
> (translation mine)

This expanded blessing/command mirrors God's stated purpose for the creation of humans as spoken in verse 26,[29] and it is connected to their

28. Bird, "'Male and Female,'" 136.

29. There are good textual reasons for suggesting that this verse is a blessing, not the least of which is the text's description of the speech: "God blessed them and said to them . . . ." But there are equally good reasons for suggesting this is a command, including the form of the verbs. Fretheim suggests understanding this as a blessing/command structure. (Fretheim, *God and the World*, 50.)

creation as the image of God. Phyllis Bird writes, "The presupposition and prerequisite for this rule is the divine stamp [image] which sets this creature apart from all the rest, identifying 'adam as God's own special representative, not simply by designation (command), but by design (nature or constitution)—as representation of God."[30] While recognizing the task of representative rule, Terence Fretheim further notes that the blessing itself indicates God's decision to share with humans his creative power. He writes, "Blessing is a word of empowerment, of divine power-sharing with the creature, which is then capable of fulfilling the named responsibilities."[31] Indeed, Fretheim indicates that it is only through God's blessing, not by their own power, that the humans will be able to be fruitful, fill, subdue, and rule the earth.[32]

The task of dominion is linked to the call to procreate in the blessing itself. "Be fruitful and increase in number; fill the earth and subdue it." Humans will have dominion over the earth as they populate the earth. The image of God will be reproduced and spread over the entire world. As they spread, they will subdue and rule, tending to the created boundaries that keep disorder at bay. No other creature is created and designed with such a specified purpose and blessed in order to execute that purpose.

Additionally, whereas other earthly creatures display a wide diversity of species "according to their kind," humans are created as a singular complex (v. 17) of male–female.

> And God created man ['adam] in his image,
> in the image of God he created him;
> male and female he created them.

The poetic structure of the text suggests that these lines cannot easily be separated from one another. Rather, these lines, especially the last two lines, indicate that God has created human persons as one, with the sexual distinction of male and female. Phyllis Bird writes, "The two parallel cola contain two essential and distinct statements about the nature of humanity:

---

30. Bird, "'Male and Female,'" 138. Bird argues here that this is a progressive parallelism where the second line does not just repeat or describe the first but adds to it and expands on it.

31. Fretheim, *God and the World*, 50. There seems to be little debate in the literature on this point. Whatever else fruitfulness might be, it is at least, in the Hebrew mind, procreation and should be understood as a gift from God, in keeping with God's blessing on the couple. See for example, Walton, *Genesis*, 109; Bird, "'Male and Female,'" 147n47.

32. Fretheim, *God and the World*, 50.

adam is created *like* (i.e., resembling) God, but *as* creature, and hence male and female."[33] In other words, as a purposeful part of the orderly creation, humans are created as male and female.

Phyllis Trible also notes this distinctive feature of humans as sexual beings. She writes, "Procreation is shared with the animal world (1:22, 28); sexuality is not."[34] Trible's point is not that the writer of Genesis did not understand biology and know that animals were also male and female. Rather, her point is that the text itself differentiates between living things. Most living things are created "after their kinds" but not described as differentiated sexually as male and female. Humans stand out as beings who are sexually created as male and female, a cohesive unit in the image of God. And of course, sexual differentiation is necessary for fulfilling the command to be fruitful and multiply.

By the end of Genesis 1, with the creation of the first couple as male and female and creation itself complete, God declares the whole of his creation is "very good" (v. 31). The repetition of "it is good" throughout the narrative, combined with the final pronouncement of God that this well-ordered world is "very good," leads to the conclusion that goodness appears, at least in some sense, correlated to God's established order. Whitekettle notes that this declaration of "very good" "implies that there is a moral order to the world (that is, that the things God has created are acting or functioning in the way that He wants them to)."[35]

Juxtaposed with this account of creation stands what may be understood to be a complementary account of creation beginning in Genesis 2:4.[36] Here the goodness of creation is melded with images of harmony and well-being that result in a vivid picture of humans in the ideal world of the Garden of Eden. The garden is depicted as a well-watered land with lush

33. Bird, "'Male and Female,'" 149.

34. Trible, *God and the Rhetoric of Sexuality*, 15.

35. Whitekettle, "Marriage Equality and the Bible." See also Brueggemann, *Theology of the Old Testament*, 338; Knight "Cosmogony and Order," 145; Vanden Berg, "Christ's Atonement," 46–51.

36. As noted earlier, Fretheim asserts that the two accounts are intended to be read together, to interact with each other, in order to offer a canonical perspective on creation. He writes, "The differing theological voices of the tradition, woven together, have become a more sophisticated theological perspective on creation and more closely approximate the understanding that Israel, finally, discerned regarding Creator and creature and their interrelationship." Fretheim, *God and the World*, 33. See also Collins, *Reading Genesis Well*, 168; Brueggemann, *Genesis*, 40.

vegetation fed by the Pishon, Gihon, Tigris, and Euphrates Rivers. Trees are provided that are both "pleasing to the eye and good for food" (Gen 2:9).

As with Genesis 1, in this account, God is said to have made the earth and heavens. But the details of this "making" are considerably different. Here God makes the world but apparently there are as of yet no plants, because God has not sent rain. Nor is anyone available in the first few verses to "work the ground." In a number of ways God seems more intimately involved in the goings on of the creative process here. *He* sends rain and *he* causes streams to come and water the ground (vv. 4–6) in a way that sounds much like Psalm 104. God does not create by speaking in this chapter but acts in a more hands-on way, anthropomorphically "forming" animals and birds out of the ground (v. 19).

The same is true with the creation of humans. Like Genesis 1, however, the text offers a few more details about the formation of humans than its description of the creation of animals. Here, unlike Genesis 1, human formation is mentioned before that of the animals and birds. Like Genesis 1, however, humans seem to have a purpose. Verse 5 notes that "there was no man (*'adam*) to work the ground (*ha'adamah*)." God subsequently forms man (*ha'adam*) from the dust of the ground (*ha'adamah*), breathing life into him so that he becomes a living being (*nephesh hayah*). The creation of humans for the purpose of working the earth, implied in verse 5, is made explicit in verse 15. Here, God places the man in the Garden of Eden "to work it and take care of it."[37] In contrast to Genesis 1, there is no mention of humans as the image of God and there is no immediate mention of a woman.

This lack of a companion, specifically the woman, is addressed in the text. As opposed to the repetitive mention of creation as "good" in Genesis 1, here God's first speech indicates that something is "not good" (v. 18); it is not good that the man is alone. Despite an unblemished relationship with his Creator, the man needs a "suitable helper," someone "like-opposite" him.[38] The other creatures present are, quite clearly, not suitable. As Brueggemann writes, "The 'help' the man needs and must have will be

---

37. Literally, to "work" or to "serve" it and to "guard" or "protect" it. These connotations when read with the harsher language of the text of Genesis 1:28 should militate against any ideas that humans have license to abuse the creation through their ruling of it. Just the opposite is the case. See Walton, *Genesis*, 113–16.

38. Hebrew: *kenegdow*; Wenham points out that if mere identity was what was intended here, "the more natural phrase would be 'like him.'" Wenham, *Genesis 1–15*, 68.

found among the 'earthlings.'"[39] Given the explicit idea of reproduction associated with the blessing on the first couple in Genesis 1, it follows that this companion must be able to serve with *ha'adam* not only as a general helper and companion, but also as a reproductive partner for the purpose of ruling the earth. John Walton writes, "The instinctive urges associated with the blessing lead him to seek out a reproductive partner."[40] In other words, the creation of *ha'adam*'s companion as female in Genesis 2 is central to understanding the overarching purpose for the creation of humans as indicated in Genesis 1:26. The man's relationship with the animals seems peaceful as he encounters each one and assigns their names. Yet none can provide the intimate companionship and potential fertility this human was created for, so God provides a woman to complement the man and complete the scene.[41] The man now has a companion uniquely suited for him. The woman is his equal, his partner in ruling over and tending the garden. "In God's garden, as God wills it, there is *mutuality and equity*," writes Bruggemann.[42] The peaceful fertility symbolizes God's presence in and blessing on this beautiful garden.[43] There is no evil and no human suffering and death. God puts the man in the garden to work it and take care of it (Gen 2:15), but apparently that work is pleasant and without pain.

The picture of creation offered in the first two chapters of Genesis is one of goodness and harmonious living. Walter Brueggemann writes that "the place of the garden is for this covenanted human community of solidarity, trust, and well-being."[44] Within this picture, then, the humans play a central and unique role. They are set apart both by the details of how they are made, and by the text's clear indication of the purpose for which they are made. No other creature has a stated purpose and is formed to execute that specific purpose. No other creature is depicted as being in an interpersonal relationship with its Creator. No other creature is identified as a sexually diverse unity. No other creature is created as the image of God.

39. Brueggemann, *Genesis*, 47.

40. Walton, *Genesis*, 143.

41. It is interesting to note that while it may seem self-evident that the man would not find a companion in the various animals, the prohibition in Leviticus 18 against bestiality seems to be connected to this fundamental boundary between animals and humans laid out first in Genesis 1 and again here in Genesis 2. Of course it also draws attention to the Creator-creature distinction.

42. Bruggemann, *Genesis*, 51.

43. Wenham, *Genesis*, 61.

44. Brueggemann, *Genesis*, 47.

The story of creation given us in Genesis 1–2 features humans as specially unique beings in at least these ways. We will now explore more deeply what is perhaps the most important unique feature of humans, their creation in the image of God.

Image of God

Within the history of Christian thinking about what makes humans unique, perhaps no topic has more written about it than the doctrine of the image of God. As noted above, the image of God is one aspect of the account of God's creation of humans that sets them apart from the rest of creation. No other creature is said to be created in the image of God. While creation as a whole reflects God as a painting reflects the artist, only humans are described as creatures who are themselves the image (*tselem*) and likeness of God.

Despite the importance of this topic in theological anthropology, there are very few references in Scripture to the image of God. In fact, the language of "image of God" is mentioned only three times in the Old Testament: in Genesis 1:26, 27, and 9:6. It is referred to somewhat more frequently in the New Testament, including at least Romans 8:29, 2 Corinthians 3:18 and 4:4, Colossians 1:5, Hebrews 1:3, and James 3:9. Furthermore, none of these texts offers an extended description of what this language might mean. The texts simply state that humans are the image/likeness of God, or that Christ is the image/likeness of God, or that humans are in the process of being transformed into the image of Christ. What Scripture is clear about is that to be a human is to be an image of God,[45] and that to be an image of God confers on humans a special place or status within the creation order. Even if all of the differences between the creation of humans and the creation of animals in the story recorded in Genesis 1–2 are not enough to convince

---

45. I take it that to be a human is to be a member of the species *homo sapiens sapiens*, the only living species of the genus *homo*. Basic to human nature are questions like the following: Who am I? What is my purpose? What does it mean to be human? The questions themselves set humans apart from any other creature. Even the highest primates who are able to function in many humanlike ways do not contemplate the meaning of their own existence. What does it mean to be a gorilla? This is not something gorillas or any other mammal contemplates so far as we know. Only humans, members of the species *homo sapiens sapiens* have the potential to transcend themselves and contemplate questions of being and purpose and meaningful living.

some that humans are specially unique within the created order, the language of "image of God" surely adds weight to the argument.

This claim is not uncontested, however. A number of scholars have written about human domination of animals and animal rights, specifically the problem of animal suffering at the hands of humans. In this context some have raised the question of the place of humans in creation and wondered about the assumed hierarchy of humans over animals.[46] Some have gone beyond these important issues and questioned whether animals should be included as the image of God.[47] We can grant that questions regarding how humans have exercised their dominion and the influence of various theologies on that role are helpful and important. However, suggesting that animals, too, are the image of God takes more than a little textual imagination. Although references to the image of God are infrequent, they are nevertheless only used with reference to humans, and never with reference to animals.

There is little consensus within theology on what is meant when humans are referred to as the image of God. Various theories have come and gone in the history of interpretation and in the history of theology as a whole.[48] That said, among biblical scholars there is relative consensus about how best to understand this phrase. The Hebrew word for image (*tselem*) most often refers to an idol. In the culture of the ancient Near East, in which Genesis 1 is situated, images (idols) were understood as representatives of the gods. Drawing on the literature of the ancient Near East, Gordon Wenham notes that this idea of an image as divine representative "was a common oriental view of the king."[49] Stephen Herring deepens this notion of representation, noting that certain ancient Near Eastern rituals would render the image "an extension or manifestation of the referent."[50] Crispin Fletcher-Louis also affirms the idea of image as representative in the ancient Near East, writing that a cultic image of a god was thought of as the "real presence and visible form of the god."[51] Understood in this con-

---

46. For example, McFarlane, "Living Relationally," 235–44; Bauckham, *Living with Other Creatures*, 1–62.

47. See, for example, Cunningham, "Way of All Flesh," 100–117; Putz, "Moral Apes," 613–24.

48. For a reasonably good discussion of this history see Cortez, *Theological Anthropology*, 18–30.

49. Wenham, *Genesis 1–15*, 30. See Daniel 3:1 for a biblical example of this.

50. Herring, "'Transubstantiated' Humanity," 489.

51. Fletcher-Louis, "God's Image," 84.

text, Genesis 1 presents humans as divine representatives. Wenham writes, "The image makes [humanity] God's representative on earth."[52] What is unique in the Genesis account versus other ancient Near Eastern accounts is that *all* humans, not just the king, are depicted as representatives of God. Furthermore, Fletcher-Lewis notes that humanity as the image of God "is given both the freedom of the cosmos, is entitled to be fed from its produce, is to fill it with God's presence, and is to exercise the creator's own divine rule over his creation (Gen 1:28–29)."[53] The exercise of divine rule is, of course, exactly what God states as his purpose for creating humans in his image: "so that they may rule" (Gen 1:26).

Richard Middleton writes that this idea of divine representation and rule is the predominant view in Old Testament biblical scholarship. He explains, "the *imago dei* designates the royal office or calling of human beings as God's representatives and agents in the world, granted authorized power to share in God's rule or administration of the earth's resources and creatures."[54] He later affirms that the connection between image of God and rule is "unquestionable" in the text.[55] Middleton concludes that from the perspective of Genesis 1, the term "image of God" is best understood through a "royal-functional" reading of the text, with humans "called to imitate or continue God's own twofold creative activity by populating and organizing (in a manner appropriate to humans) the unformed and unfilled earth."[56] In the creation of humans, God has, Middleton writes, "started the process of forming and filling, which humans, as God's earthly delegates, are to continue."[57] Humans are God's royal delegates, those, as Anthony Hoekema writes, through whom God "works out his purposes on earth."[58] Not only does this royal-functional understanding confer on humanity incredible dignity, but also incredible responsibility—a dignity and responsibility that is not shared with any other creature.

52. Wenham, *Genesis 1–15*, 30.

53. Fletcher-Louis, "God's Image," 84.

54. Middleton, *Liberating Image*, 24–27.

55. Middleton, *Liberating Image*, 50. For his complete discussion of the connection of image and rule, see pp. 50–55.

56. Middleton, *Liberating Image*, 88–89.

57. Middleton, *Liberating Image*, 89.

58. Hoekema, *Created in God's Image*, 68.

Other Biblical Texts

While Genesis 1–2 and the description of the image of God certainly deserve primacy of place in any consideration of human uniqueness in Scripture, too often the discussions of humans and their place in creation end there. As we look across Scripture, both Old and New Testaments, various descriptions and themes begin to emerge, in addition to those already noted in the creation story of Genesis 1–2. Many of these themes identify humans as both like and unlike the rest of creation, while some also point to the special uniqueness of humans.

Psalm 8 is a good place to begin the broader foray into Scripture. This well-known psalm not only offers a beautiful picture of the special uniqueness of humans within creation, but also repeats many of the themes of Genesis 1:27–30. The psalm begins and ends with praise of YHWH, but the intervening lines focus almost entirely on humanity. In verses 3–4 the psalmist ponders God's care of humans and God's remembering them, bringing them to mind. God is depicted as attentive to humans in this psalm in ways that are different from God's providential care of the rest of creation. As to the human place in creation, verse 5 notes that humans are a "little lower than the heavenly beings" and crowned with glory and honor. The word translated in the NIV as "heavenly beings" (*elohim*) might also be translated "gods," "god," or "God." In other words, this psalm could be understood as saying that humans are made a little lower than the one true God, that they are Godlike.[59] If we put this in parallel with the unique features of humans given in Genesis 1, it is not a far stretch to suggest that whatever else it is to be the image of God, it is to be crowned with glory and honor. What could give more honor to a creature than to be made like its Creator, the One whose name is "majestic in all the earth"? In addition, Psalm 8 reiterates the purpose for which humans were made—to rule. God has made humans the rulers over everything in creation (vv. 6–7). Humans, in other words, have an exalted place within the creation, both by design and vocation.

As noted above, Psalm 8 offers a glimpse of God's special care for and attentiveness toward humans. This idea of God's conscientious care of humans is pervasive throughout the Psalter. One prime example of this is Psalm 139. Carolyn Pressler points out that this psalm is centered "solidly

---

59. See Middleton, *Liberating Image*, 58.

within the context of an 'I-Thou,' or, rather, a 'Thou-I' relationship."[60] God's intimate knowledge of everything about the psalmist is highlighted in the first few verses with the repeated use of the verb "know" (*yada*), as well as verbs like discern, sift through, and be familiar with.[61] God is portrayed in this prayer as "knowing" and "examining" the psalmist. This intimacy between the human subject and God is both beautiful and disturbing.

The psalmist's knowledge of God's intimate knowing of him is not as comforting as one might expect. Rather, it is ambiguous as indicated by the psalmist's desire to flee. The psalm makes clear that God knows everything about the psalmist, even what he intends to say before he says it. If we put ourselves into the psalmist's shoes, then, can we blame him for his desire to run and hide? The psalmist is comprehensively known by YHWH, who is both gracious and a consuming fire. As Pressler writes, "The psalmist experiences the inescapable presence of God as possibly salvific, but also as potentially threatening."[62]

While this psalm is perhaps the most dramatic portrayal of the interpersonal nature of the relationship between humans and God, the basic depiction of humans as beings created for relationship, especially a relationship with God, is a central theme of Scripture. The gift of the Psalms is their unique look at the emotional outworking of this relationship, both individually and corporately. John Calvin rightly refers to the Psalter as "an anatomy of all parts of the soul," going on to note that "there is not an emotion of which anyone can be conscious that is not here represented as in a mirror."[63] In the Psalms, humans praise God, rejoice in God, and sing to God, for example. But humans also cry out to God in despair and call on God, who at times seems absent. God is expected to respond with salvation, mercy, and love, but sometimes also with wrath and destruction of enemies. The call and response of this relationship is assumed. In the Psalter, humans are depicted calling on God with the general assurance that God will, at least eventually, answer.

That God intends for humans to have a relationship with him is especially apparent in his establishment of a covenant with his people. In the garden, humans rebel against God, choosing autonomy rather than relationship with their Creator. They even attempt to avoid God's pursuit of

60. Pressler, "Certainty, Ambiguity, and Trust," 92.

61. Pressler, "Certainty, Ambiguity, and Trust," 92.

62. Pressler, "Certainty, Ambiguity, and Trust," 93.

63. Calvin, *Commentary on the Book of Psalms*, xxxvii.

relationship with them by hiding. This breach in the human relationship with God has consequences that reverberate throughout history. Biblically, the effects are observed spiraling out of control in Genesis 4–11. God responds to the ongoing rebellion portrayed in these chapters by calling Abram into a relationship with him and sealing that relationship with a covenant (Gen 12:1–3; 15; 17). The covenant guarantees the endurance of the relationship to all of Abram's descendants who acknowledge YHWH as Lord. The purpose of this renewed relationship is the blessing of all people. In other words, Abram and his descendants will mediate God's blessing to the world, once again offering rebellious humanity the opportunity to have a relationship with their Creator just as God intended. Humans are created with the capacity for relationship with God, and this is so important that God himself will ensure that the relationship is maintained. As N. T. Wright has suggested, a loving, interpersonal relationship with humanity has been God's plan from the beginning.[64] While all of creation will find relief from the effects of human rebellion, the redemption of humans' relationship with God is what will lead the way to the renewal of all things.[65] Indeed, the central purpose of the incarnation, death, and resurrection of the Son of God is the restoration of the human relationship with God. Now, following this Christ-event, the veil between God and humans is torn so that we can "approach the throne of grace with confidence" (Heb 4:16).

Covenant relationship with God implies another unique feature of humans. Scripture presents humans as moral beings; animals, by contrast, are not portrayed as moral beings. While all creatures are expected to operate within their divinely given creational parameters, only humans are given specific laws to which their will and behavior must conform in order to maintain their relationship with God and the rest of creation. As Brueggemann writes, "The destiny of the human creature is to live in God's world, with God's other creatures, *on God's terms.*"[66] This is as true in the first chapters of Genesis as it is in the Psalms, the Prophets, and the New Testament. And while the written law does not come into view until the book of Exodus, the orderliness of creation itself is related to the moral law, thus living "on God's terms" entails living within the boundaries of creation itself.

64. Wright, "Big Picture."

65. See Vanden Berg, "Christ's Atonement," 10–15, 180–91; Bolt, "Relation between Creation and Redemption," 35; Wright, "Letter to the Romans," 596.

66. Brueggemann, *Genesis*, 40. Emphasis original.

These implicit laws of the creation order become explicit in the covenant stipulations given at Sinai. Everything from the Ten Commandments and the ritual laws of Leviticus to the reiteration of the law in Deuteronomy and even to the various commands given by Jesus and his followers in the New Testament are intended to keep humans pointed toward the purpose of living in right relationship with God and others. No other animal is given explicit commands and assumed by Scripture to have the ability to make a moral choice to obey or disobey these commands. For humans, to disobey these commands and turn away from God is to be a fool or senseless or lack understanding.[67] In fact, Isaiah suggests that when humans rebel against God's laws, they prove themselves to have less understanding than an ox or donkey (Isa 1:3). Unlike animals, humans are responsible for their moral behavior, particularly their rebellion against God. From a biblical perspective, animals do not sin and do not rebel against their maker. Only humans are prone to this self-destructive behavior.

In the same vein, only humans are depicted as punishable by God for their wrongdoing.[68] Creation as a whole suffers because of human rebellion against God already with the first sin. God says to Adam and Eve, "Cursed is the ground because of you" (Gen 3:17).[69] But humans are directly punished. This is not just true of the first sin, but of all subsequent sin. Human sin merits God's judgment. Indeed, the covenant stipulations include not just blessing for those who keep the covenant, but curses for those who do not.

Spiritual-Material Beings

So humans are specially unique, unlike the rest of the material creation and set apart from it by virtue of how they are created, the purpose for which they are created, their calling into and interpersonal relationship with their

67. See, for example, Ps 14:1; Isa 44:16–20; Jer 4:22; 5:4; 10:8.

68. One exception is the case in Exod 21:28, where God instructs Israel to put to death an ox that has gored a person to death. However, most commentators agree that this is not an instance of holding an animal morally responsible for human death. See for example, Durham, *Exodus*, 325; Brueggemann, "Exodus," 865. Propp, however, does suggest that animals can bear guilt, citing Gen 9:4–5. Propp, *Exodus 19–40*, 233. My own sense is that Scripture says very little directly about animal moral responsibility so it is unlikely that these obscure texts support animal morality.

69. For a particularly interesting connection between human sin and the resulting suffering of creation, see Hos 4:1–3.

Creator, and their moral responsibility for their actions. One last aspect of human special uniqueness drawn from Scripture is worth pointing out. Humans are depicted as material-spiritual beings. Although the concept of a soul has come under criticism in recent years in biblical, theological, philosophical, and scientific circles, for most of the history of the church this was not the case.

The idea of the soul was simply standard doctrine for most of church history. Some have criticized this as a Greek infiltration of the church born from the science of Plato and Aristotle. While the early church was almost certainly influenced by Greek philosophy and science, it is not at all clear that this influence countered their own understanding of the received tradition of Scripture. It is no more likely that Greek ideas were slavishly accepted by early theologians than that current scientific notions are slavishly accepted by contemporary theologians.[70]

Regardless of a Greek influence, the question is at this point whether the idea of a soul is biblical. Unfortunately, the "soul," especially following Descartes, has become freighted with all sorts of connotations, including the assumption that affirmation of a soul entails a strong substance dualism. But this is not the case. Aquinas, for example, was not a strong substance dualist in the Cartesian sense, yet he did affirm a soul, as was explained in the previous chapter. So part of the problem with considering whether the soul is a biblical concept lies in what is meant by the word "soul." In asking the question about whether the idea of a soul is biblical, particularly with respect to the Old Testament, I want to be clear that I am not investigating, in some sort of anachronistic way, whether Greek conceptions of the soul were in the mind of the authors of the Old Testament. Rather, what I am asking is whether Scripture affirms that humans, as holistic beings, have an immaterial component that is included in that whole along the lines of what Aquinas proposes.

To that question, I think the answer is yes for several reasons. One reason has to do with the Hebrew word *nephesh,* often translated as "soul,"

---

70. In my opinion, however, due to a general decline in biblical knowledge and a reduction in the number of theologians who affirm the authority of Scripture, it seems much more likely that current theology is overly influenced by modern science and the empiricism that underlies it than that ancient theologians let their exegetical concerns be unduly influenced by Platonic or Aristotelian ideas. After all, the earliest decades of the church were marked by persecution, something Christians in the West today know almost nothing about. Thus, it seems implausible that the early Christians would compromise biblical truth to be in vogue with the culture of the day.

but which includes a wide range of meanings, including "life," "person," "blood," "throat," and many more.[71] Around the beginning of the twentieth century, scholars began to question whether "soul" was a proper translation of this word. In part, this was because "soul" was used to translate nearly all instances of the word *nephesh* in the Old Testament, a word that occurs more than 750 times. In some instances that was not the best translation.[72] These apparent mistranslations led the scholarship of the day to insist that Scripture presented only a monistic account of human persons. As Richard Pleijel explains, "The Bible, it was said, knows nothing about a human 'soul' in contrast to the human body."[73] However, Pleijel goes on to argue, the fact that in *some* places *nephesh* should not be translated as "soul," should not have overturned *every* instance where *nephesh* was translated "soul." Indeed, after surveying a number of texts, Pleijel concludes the following:

> The Ancient Hebrews *differentiated* between [*nephesh*] and the person connected to it. Thus, the [*nephesh*] is perceived in a number of instances in the Hebrew Bible as an entity separable, and indeed separated, from the human body. Hence, in these instances it cannot be equated with the human person, as the monistic interpretation argues.[74]

In other words, while "soul" as conceived of by the Greeks may not be a legitimate conception for the Hebrews, the word *nephesh* as used in various places in the Old Testament suggests that Israel did have some sort of a conception of a spiritual aspect of human persons that was separable from the body.

The idea of a soul that is separable from the body is most often associated with the death of the person. One frequently overlooked reason for affirming some conception of a soul that is separable from the body is Israel's cultural context. If, as some suggest, Israel had no notion of a conscious, disembodied afterlife, they would have been very unusual in their ancient Near Eastern environment. Every other known culture in the ancient Near East affirmed some sort of ontologically distinct "soul" that could survive death. Richard Steiner writes that "belief in the existence—and afterlife—of

71. See, for example, Brown, Driver, and Briggs, *Hebrew and English Lexicon*, s.v. "*nephesh*"; Cooper, *Body, Soul, and Life Everlasting*, 42–43. Miller, "Hebrew Bible's Concept of Life," 223–39.

72. Pleijel, "Translating the Biblical Hebrew Word *Nephesh*," 155.

73. Pleijel, "Translating the Biblical Hebrew Word *Nephesh*," 155.

74. Pleijel, "Translating the Biblical Hebrew Word *Nephesh*," 164.

disembodied souls was extremely widespread in the ancient Near East."[75] The relationship of this "soul" to the body varied depending on the culture. One example of an immaterial disembodied existence is described by Dennis Pardee's examination and interpretation of an inscription from a funeral stele at Zincirli in modern Turkey. The likely date of this inscription, according to Pardee, is "the third quarter of the eighth century BCE."[76] This predates Platonic philosophy by several hundred years and falls roughly during the time of Assyrian dominance and the conquering of the northern kingdom of Israel.

The inscription is generally clear, although Pardee notes some ambiguities. What is important is what is described in this inscription. The "soul" of the deceased is presented as continuing to exist in the monument or stele. This "soul" or "self" eats and drinks at a feast.[77] Pardee explains that "it was obvious to all that the exterior manifestation [the stele] could neither eat nor drink, but the *nbš* within the stele was considered capable of doing so, apparently in a way similar to that in which deities ate and drank the offerings presented to them."[78] He goes on to note that "being" is probably a good translation of this immaterial self that continues to exist.

Another example in the ancient Near East of the belief in a "soul" comes from Egypt. Micaela Bauks notes that much of what we know about Egyptian conceptions of human persons comes from their description of the afterlife. "It is striking," she writes, "that it is not in a creation context, but rather in the cult of the afterlife that we find a concern regarding the nature of the human being."[79] In other words, as with the Zincirli text, the depictions of the Egyptian afterlife offer helpful insight into Egyptian anthropology, particularly postmortem existence. Egyptian funerary practices, including depictions of the journey and the judgment of the dead, are described in detail in many Egyptian tombs. Bauks explains that the afterlife depicts three distinct ideas of a nonphysical "self" or "soul" that continues to exist after death, the *b3*, the *k3*, and the *'kh*.[80] Of most importance for our purposes is the *ba* or *b3*. "Every man has a *b3*, which is

---

75. Steiner, *Disembodied Souls*, 21.
76. Pardee, "New Aramaic Inscription," 51.
77. Pardee, "New Aramaic Inscription," 62–63.
78. Pardee, "New Aramaic Inscription," 63.
79. Bauks, "'Soul Concepts,'" 185.
80. Bauks, "'Soul Concepts,'" 185.

spiritual rather than physical, and which lives on after the body has died."[81] While Egyptian anthropology is complex, it is clear that they had not only a robust understanding of the afterlife, but also an assumption that this afterlife was experienced by the spiritual aspect of a person—what we might call the soul. In other words, it is clear that the Egyptians, like other cultures in the ancient Near East, had a well-developed belief in a spiritual aspect of humans that continued to exist postmortem.[82]

Given the evidence that cultures in the ancient Near East generally affirmed some sort of ongoing immaterial postmortem existence, it seems odd that scholars have embraced the idea that Israel did not have such a belief. Was Israel, surrounded as she was by these cultures throughout her history, immune to these beliefs when she so readily adopted other beliefs of the nations around her, including beliefs and practices that were forbidden? In addition, given that four hundred years of her history of becoming a nation happened in Egypt, and given the fairly robust Egyptian conception of a "soul" that survives death, it seems implausible to think that Israel did not come out of Egypt with some sort of notion of an ongoing spiritual postmortem existence.[83] In other words, given that disembodied existence was believed by nearly every culture in the ancient Near East, there is a heavy burden of proof for those who would deny this belief for Israel. As we consider the biblical evidence, we should do so with the preunderstanding that it is considerably more likely than not that Israel shared the common cultural idea of existence beyond the death of the body.

So let us examine some biblical evidence that Israel believed in some sort of spirit or soul that continued to exist postmortem. Indirectly the prohibition against necromancy in Israel suggests belief in the ongoing existence of human persons postmortem. Necromancy is no minor offense. Deuteronomy 18:10–12 describes consulting the dead as one of a list of practices that are *to'ebah*, a word variously translated as "detestable,"

---

81. Bauks, "'Soul Concepts," 185.

82. It is important to note that while Bauks does affirm the Egyptian notion of an ongoing spiritual afterlife, she argues against the idea that Israel had any notion of a "soul." See Bauks, "'Soul Concepts," 189–93.

83. It is worth pointing out that to say someone *exists* in these contexts is not necessarily identical to saying a person *lives* after death. As Bauks points out in her essay, while Genesis 2 talks about God breathing life into the first man and him becoming a "living being," Numbers 6, using the same language (*nephesh*) to refer to a "dead being." The point overall seems to be there are various ways to understand *nephesh*. Given that is the case, why not allow the theological understanding of the church to be one of those ways?

"abomination," or "abhorrent."[84] Leviticus 19:31 and 20:6 similarly prohibit consulting with "mediums" or "spiritists," indicating that those who do will be cut off from the people of God, one of the most severe penalties in Israel. In addition, the one who practices as a medium or spiritist, according to Leviticus 20:27, will be stoned to death. All of this was tied up with unfaithfulness to YHWH.

It could be suggested that the prohibition against necromancy is itself an indication that Israel did not affirm any idea of a "soul" that continues after death. Perhaps it indicates that Israel's basic belief was purely materialistic, and any conception of a "spirit" or "soul" was an add-on from the nations around them, nations whose ways they were not to follow. Maybe. But the real problem does not seem to lie in belief in an ongoing immaterial existence for humans. Rather, the problem lies in consulting the dead for assistance instead of, or alongside of, consulting YHWH, something the Israelite culture clearly believed was possible. Isaiah makes this point: "When men tell you to consult mediums and spiritists, who whisper and mutter, should not a people inquire of their God? Why consult the dead on behalf of the living?" (Isa 8:19). The prophet is not concerned with Israel's apparent belief in "spirits" or "souls" or the ongoing life of the dead. In fact, he seems to assume that belief. He is concerned that Israel places trust in the messages of the dead rather than placing their trust in God and waiting on God for relief from their troubles. Indeed, King Saul's death is attributed to his unfaithfulness to YHWH, part of which included his consulting with a medium, the witch of Endor (1 Chr 10:13)

The story of Saul in 1 Samuel 28 is, in fact, a vivid example of consulting the dead and the penalty for that action. Earlier, in 1 Samuel 15, the prophet Samuel delivers news to Saul, whom he had anointed as king. Because Saul had rejected God's word with regard to the destruction of the Amalekites, YHWH then *rejected* him as king. By the time of the events of 1 Samuel 28, Samuel has died, and Saul is being confronted by the Philistine army. Because he is no longer God's chosen servant over Israel, even though Saul inquires of YHWH, he does not receive an answer. In desperation, he chooses to consult a dead Samuel through the "witch of Endor" rather than place his trust in YHWH. Bill Arnold, commenting on this text states, "The idea that the deceased [in these rituals] rises up out of the ground reflects the concept of Sheol as a place for the dead beneath the

---

84. Brown, Driver, and Briggs, *Hebrew and English Lexicon*, s.v. "to'ebah."

earth's surface to which people descend at death."[85] Although Sheol is not mentioned in this particular text, what is clear is that Samuel is being called from a place where people exist in some way. Indeed, Samuel says to Saul, "tomorrow you and your sons will be with me" (v. 19). In order for this story to have any meaning at all to Saul or to those Israelites who heard the story, it presupposes their assumptions that the dead continue to exist in a disembodied state.

John Cooper affirms this point, noting that the Old Testament has a word for these disembodied persons: the *rephaim*.[86] He notes especially Isaiah 14:9–10, where the dead "are able to recognize the Babylonian king, speak to him, and compare their former situations with the present."[87] In other words, at least in this text of Isaiah it appears that the dead continue to exist and are able to act to some degree. Cooper writes that this oracle "seems to indicate that occasional activity was at least in principle possible in the Hebrew view of the deceased."[88]

In addition to the idea of the *rephaim*, Richard Steiner offers substantial biblical evidence for affirmation of the ongoing existence of a disembodied *nephesh*. Steiner observes that the Old Testament descriptions of the patriarchs being "brought to their kinsman" at death is not a reference to the patriarch's burials, as is often argued. Rather, "the texts make clear," he writes, "that this occurred *before* internment," and because of this "must be speaking of a reunion of souls/spirits."[89] In addition to this argument, Steiner offers several texts that he argues locate the human *nephesh* outside of the human body. Steiner suggests that to translate *nephesh* as "life" in 1 Kings 17:22 is problematic, "since life is not an entity that can be located in space."[90] He notes that the word *hayim* (life) is never used in this way. In addition, he explains that in Psalm 116:7 the psalmist "tells [his *nephesh*] to return to its resting places, that is, its usual haunts."[91] He argues that with both 1 Kings 17 and Psalm 116 substituting "life" for "soul" does not make

85. Arnold, "Necromancy and Cleromancy," 202.

86. Cooper, *Body, Soul, and Life Everlasting*, 60.

87. Cooper, *Body, Soul, and Life Everlasting*, 63. See also Job 26:5 for another example of actions of the *rephaim*.

88. Cooper, *Body, Soul, and Life Everlasting*, 63.

89. Steiner, *Disembodied Souls*, 101.

90. Steiner, *Disembodied Souls*, 69.

91. Steiner, *Disembodied Souls*, 69.

sense given the spatial location associated with the soul in both cases.[92] In other words, not only would one expect Israel's beliefs to be in basic continuity with the nations around them, but also the Old Testament text itself confirms Israelite belief in a disembodied existence.

Citing Steiner's work, Richard Pleijel also affirms that in several instances the Old Testament describes the *nephesh* as having a spatial location. He also offers as one example the story of Elijah and the death of the son of the widow at Zarephath in 1 Kings 17.[93] The NIV translates Elijah's cry to the LORD on behalf of the son, "O LORD my God, let this boy's life [*nephesh*] return to him" (v. 21). The following verse records that "The LORD heard Elijah's cry, and the boy's life [*nephesh*] returned to him, and he lived." Pleijel argues that the NIV translation obscures what is happening here. He points out that the Hebrew text itself suggests that the boy's *nephesh* was somewhere else and then returned to him. He argues that whether the preposition 'al is understood as "into" or "upon," both translations "support the interpretation of [*nephesh*] as an independent entity in relation to the child."[94] Pleijel's overall point is not that *nephesh* should never be translated as "life" or any of the other numerous translations suggested. Rather, his point is that scholarship from the early twentieth century up to the present, in its enthusiasm to support a monistic view of human persons, has overlooked biblical data that suggest that Israel did in fact have a conception of a spiritual, separable aspect of human persons that could rightly be considered a "soul."

Based on the above arguments, declarations that suggest Israel had no conception of a "soul" are most likely an overstatement driven by something other than exegetical concerns. As far as New Testament beliefs, if, as I suggest, Israelite anthropology was not monistic but rather holistic, including a body and soul that were temporarily separable at death, then it would make sense that New Testament anthropology would be much the same.[95] That is to say, if ancient Israel believed in a disembodied afterlife of some sort, it is difficult to imagine that this belief would disappear in the

---

92. Steiner, *Disembodied Souls*, 70.

93. For additional examples, see Pleijel, "To Be or to Have a *Nephesh*," 201–3.

94. Pleijel, "To Be or to Have a *Nephesh*," 202.

95. For good biblical arguments overall, including detailed New Testament arguments for biblical support of a soul, see Cooper, *Body, Soul, and Life Everlasting.* Cooper suggests in this work the idea of holistic dualism, an idea very similar to that of Aquinas.

Greco-Roman context of the New Testament, which had a lively belief in a disembodied afterlife.

Indeed, despite ongoing debate on the subject,[96] the New Testament does affirm the idea of a spiritual aspect of humans. Jesus himself cries from the cross, "Father into your hands I commit my spirit" (Luke 23:46). Anthony Hoekema notes that this, along with the stoning of Stephen in Acts 7, is a text where "dying is described as the departure either of the soul or the spirit."[97] In the same Lukan text dealing with Jesus's crucifixion, Jesus assures the thief on the cross next to him that "today you will be with me in paradise" (Luke 23:43). Cooper argues that here "Luke clearly means for his readers to hear the same promise that Jesus made the thief: 'If you confess Jesus as the Christ, paradise is yours immediately upon your death.'"[98] Given that the thief's body is still on the cross at his death, Jesus's words assume that it is his spirit or soul that will be in "paradise."

When we move to the Pauline texts, we find further evidence for some sort of spiritual aspect of humans that survives death. In 2 Cor 5, Paul begins by describing the body as a "tent," which burdens us, along with the longing to be "clothed" with our "heavenly dwelling." He goes on to write, "We are confident and know that as long as we are at home in the body we are away from the Lord. We live by faith, not by sight. We are confident, I say, and would prefer to be away from the body and at home with the Lord" (2 Cor 5:6–8). Given Paul's Hebraic background, it makes sense that he has in mind some sort of disembodied existence. Hoekema writes that "2 Cor. 5:8 clearly teaches that human beings can exist apart from their bodies."[99] While Hoekema makes clear that the final state of humans is the resurrection of the body, he affirms that the New Testament teaches that "the state of believers between death and resurrection is one of provisional happiness, one that is 'better by far' than the present earthly state (Phil. 1:23)."[100] The New Testament does not shout on this matter of an ongoing spiritual existence post-mortem, giving almost no details about it. But it does whisper and this whisper teaches that humans are holistic, material-spiritual beings. Hoekema summarizes this well explaining that although humans enter a disembodied state at death, "the normal state of humans is

96. For counter arguments, see for example, Green, *Body, Soul, and Human Life*.

97. Hoekema, *Created in God's Image*, 207.

98. Cooper, *Body, Soul, and Life Everlasting*, 141.

99. Hoekema, *Created in God's Image*, 222.

100. Hoekema, *Created in God's Image*, 220.

one of psychosomatic unity. At the time of the resurrection he or she will be fully restored to that unity and will once again be made complete."[101]

In general, while it remains controversial, the biblical argument for a soul is nonetheless plausible and defensible, particularly when framed within the culture of the ancient Near East and the first century church. The Bible does not necessarily and clearly reject the notion of a "soul." Conversely, it seems, at the very least, to allow for it and likely even affirms it when we add the New Testament data, especially the Pauline texts, into the picture.[102]

Conclusion

So what have we learned from Scripture about the special uniqueness of human persons? First, we learned that the grammar and syntax of the first chapter of Genesis sets the creation of human persons apart from that of the rest of creation. Beginning with God's self-deliberation about humans, God is portrayed as taking a special interest in this particular being. Humans have a stated purpose and are directly addressed by God, blessed in order to fulfill this purpose. In addition, humans are created in the image of God. While some have suggested that other beings might also be considered the image of God, the arguments for that viewpoint are arguments from silence. Nowhere does Scripture state that beings other than humans are made in his image, like God in certain ways and charged to represent him. Scripture also depicts humans as created for a special relationship with God. God intimately knows humans, and humans personally and emotionally interact with God. This interpersonal relationship between God and humans is related to humans as moral beings. Humans are intended to live within the parameters God gives them and failure to do so entails not only punishment, but an inability to enjoy the fullness of life as God intended. Finally, this chapter has argued that Scripture at least allows for a holistic-dualist conception of humans, the idea that humans are spiritual-material beings. While I am not suggesting a perfect match between the material we have studied in this chapter and Aquinas's anthropology, it should be clear that everything from his hierarchy of being, which places humans

101. Hoekema, *Created in God's Image*, 222.

102. For more on this, see Cooper, *Body, Soul, and the Life Everlasting*, 104–72. Cooper offers an excellent, comprehensive summary of New Testament texts that implicate or directly affirm the idea of a disembodied, conscious postmortem existence.

near the top and distinct in both form and function from other beings, to his conception of humans as a body-soul unity fits quite nicely with the biblical material we have examined. In the following chapter, we will take a look at what scientific data might have to tell us about whether humans may be considered specially unique.

3

Humans and Other Animals

Up to this point, we have examined Aquinas's Treatise on Human Nature as one way that the Christian tradition has considered where humans fit in the created order. While giving preference to "sacred doctrine," Aquinas uses the science of his day—that is, the writings of Aristotle—as well as philosophical tools to offer a portrait of humans and their place in the world. Aquinas makes clear that humans are unique in a variety of ways. These features or capacities are part of what is entailed in being human.

We then dug deep into Scripture to determine whether it presents humans as specially unique. We noted several ways that Scripture sets humans apart from the rest of creation. First, the language and syntax of the story of human origins in Genesis 1 signals humans as specially unique within the creation order. Second, humans are presented as the image of God, a description given to no other creature. Third, humans are the only creature that are created for a specific purpose, that of ruling the creation. Fourth, Scripture as a whole presents humans as related to God in a unique way that is not characteristic of the rest of creation. Humans are consistently shown as beings not just situated in relation to God, but created for interpersonal relationship with their Creator, both individually and communally, as covenant suggests. To put it in the words of an old song, only humans have a relationship with God that could be poetically described as God "walks with me and talks with me and tells me I am his own," a central feature of the covenantal relationship between God and humans. So far, nothing we have examined should cause much anxiety with respect to our understanding of humans, because for the most part, it all falls in line with what has been taught throughout most of church history in one form or another.

The overall discussion of human uniqueness with which this book is concerned may begin to cause more anxiety as we turn to how science approaches the question of human uniqueness. In their examination of the physical world through the lenses of the physical and behavioral sciences, both of which work within an evolutionary framework, scientists can offer insights into where humans fit in the world. Specifically, scientists are well-equipped to help us see through their specialized lens how humans as we observe them today are both like and unlike the rest of creation. Their work can help us understand whether, apart from what Scripture tells us, humans are in fact specially unique.

Human Similarity to Other Creatures

It is not particularly unusual to notice similarities between various primates and humans. Jane Goodall did more than perhaps any other scientist to emphasize these similarities. While we will get to the similarities between humans and other primates, we will start by considering humans within the larger taxonomy or classification of creatures. Scientists group creatures together by similar features. Specifically, Ian Tattersall explains, "There is now a whole range of computer-based routines for generating statements of relationship among groups of organisms, using diverse data sets ranging from morphological and even behavioral character states to DNA structure."[1] There are various levels in this taxonomy going from the broadest level of similarity to the most specific level of similarity. The broadest taxonomic level is called the "domain." Then, in order, comes the kingdom, phylum, class, order, family, genus, and species.[2] Within each level the rules for entrance, that is, the features that distinguish each particular taxon, become more and more precise. By the time we get to the level of species, the differences between species are great enough that different species cannot successfully interbreed.

Geologist Harold Levin illustrates taxonomy using humans as his example. He writes:

---

1. Tattersall, *Paleontology*, 37.
2. Levin, *Earth through Time*, 132.

To use yourself as an example, you are a member of the following:

Domain	Eukarya (organisms having one or more cells that contain visible nuclei)
Kingdom	Animalia (animals)
Phylum	Chordata (animals that have a backbone)
Class	Mammalia (warm-blooded animals that have fur and suckle their young)
Order	Primates (mammals, comprising humans, apes, monkeys)
Family	Hominidae (African apes and humans)
Genus	*Homo* (human)
Species	*sapiens* (wise)[3]

Several rather obvious things are worth noting. First, whatever species one is examining, that species is, by virtue of being a species, unique in its own right. Thus, the reminder that what this book is looking for is not human uniqueness as such, but what we identified early on as humans being *specially* unique. In other words, it is not simply that humans are distinct from other beings in certain ways. That could be said of any species. The point is that humans have a different level of distinction from other species that sets them apart as specially unique.

Second, regardless of the species one is considering, it should be obvious from the taxonomy that all species share some level of similarity with other species in their domain, with the understanding that this similarity is due to relatedness.[4] It is also the case that as data accumulate, taxonomy changes, rearranging the branches on family trees. As an example, consider Tattersall's description of vertebrates, a sub-phylum of chordates. Vertebrates

> are chordates with backbones that not only enclose and protect the nerve cord, but are composed of complex vertebrae. The vertebrates also have an elaborate circulatory system powered by a heart, a brain at the front end of the neural cord, complex paired eyes with single lenses, and a unique form of embryological development involving primordial neural crest cells that migrate out

---

3. Levin, *Earth through Time,* 132.

4. It is the case that modern taxonomy and phylogenetics aim to group together closely related organisms. Accumulated data, therefore, may actually rearrange the branches on family trees, thus changing the taxonomy. Thank you to Dr. Ryan Bebej for helping me learn more about this.

from the nerve cord to control the development of many aspects of the body.[5]

If this description sounds familiar to you, it should. You should be able to identify with all of the features listed in this description, even if you aren't sure what all of them are. Now pause for a moment, and go back to Levin's taxonomy. Where is "Chordata" situated? It is part of the level called "phylum." Note that this is only the third category down the list of taxa. Many of the creatures classified as vertebrates within Chordata would not immediately come to mind as organisms that bear similarity to humans. For example, a guppy, a turtle, and a snake are all vertebrates. Likely as not, being compared to at least one of those things would be considered an insult for most people—my grandchildren being a glaring exception.

The important point to grasp in considering the taxonomy of humans as described by Levin is that humans bear some similarity to many, many other creatures. We could begin at the broadest level, the "domain," and note that humans, like other creatures in Eukarya, have cells that contain a nucleus that is visible, have a cell membrane, and contains the genetic material for the cell. Humans share this nuclear structure with plants, as well as any number of other organisms. If we move to the next level, "kingdom," plants are no longer included. Humans inhabit the kingdom called "Animalia," or animals. We share any number of features with other animals, even really strange animals. For example, all animals are made up of more than one cell. That may seem like a rather low standard, sort of like saying that a house must have walls, but that is a central identifying feature of animals.

If we chose, we could continue to work down the entire taxonomy that Levin presented and find various features that humans share in each category with others in that particular category. More interesting, however, is to jump down a few categories to the order of primates, which is where the similarities begin to get interesting. Humans share the primate order with, to name several common creatures, lemurs, monkeys, marmosets, baboons, orangutans, and gorillas. Think for a moment about the last time you visited a zoo. What did you think as you saw one of these animals playing or grooming or maybe even looking at you? It is difficult not to notice that many of the characteristics of these creatures are similar to human features.

If we move one more level down Levin's hierarchy to the family Hominidae, the monkeys and lemurs and other of the primates with tails

5. Tattersall, *Paleontology*, 41.

disappear. This group consists of our closest evolutionary relatives, the great apes. Two living relatives that we share a common ancestor with are the chimpanzee and the pygmy chimpanzee, known as the bonobo. Within the Hominidae family, humans are members of the genus *Homo*, while the chimpanzee and the bonobo are members of the genus *Pan*. The fact that we are members of the same family bears witness to substantial similarity between these animals and humans.

Some similarities are quite obvious, the sort you observe at the zoo. Chimpanzees and bonobos have a body structure and facial features similar to those of humans. I think it is fair to say that overall the physical features of these creatures are more humanlike than any other creature. Thomas Suddendorf notes that when apes were first brought to Europe, people were so surprised by their similarity to humans that "they were often considered half man and half beast."[6] The names given to apes reflected this assessment. For example, in German, "apes are known as Menschenaffen."[7] Outward appearances alone, in other words, suggest a close evolutionary relationship. Digging down into the cells of chimpanzees, bonobos, and humans yields even more striking similarities. Chimpanzees and bonobos share about 99.6 percent of each other's DNA. In addition, both chimpanzees and bonobos share about 98.7 percent of their DNA with humans.[8] In numbers, this genetic gap between humans and our nearest evolutionary relatives amounts to about 40 million differences in our DNA.[9] In addition, bonobos, chimpanzees, and humans are all more closely related to each other than to the giant apes like gorillas and orangutans.[10]

Even more interesting than these physical similarities are some of the observed behavioral similarities. Humans have frequently been described as toolmaking animals. As it turns out, chimpanzees are toolmakers too. Byrne explains that chimpanzees make a number of different tools for a variety of purposes. It is clear, he writes, "that they have an approximate *design* in mind in each case, a schematic anticipation of the tool—a plan

---

6. Suddendorf, *Gap*, 18.

7. Suddendorf, *Gap*, 18. The German word *Menschenaffen* is a compound of two words—*Menschen*, which is plural for human, and *Affen*, which is plural for ape. Thus these animals were literally called "human-apes."

8. Gibbons, "Bonobos Join Chimps."

9. Wolchover, "Chimps vs. Humans."

10. De Waal, *Peacemaking among Primates*, 172.

in mind."[11] In other words, many animals use rocks or sticks to accomplish some task. Chimpanzees, however, actually fashion tools for a particular purpose. Byrne offers this example about how chimpanzees go about acquiring a meal of termites who nest fifty centimeters under the floor of the forest and whose tunnels cannot be excavated:

> The first tool needed is a probe: to locate a nest and make an access route to it. For this, Goualougo chimpanzees use a sturdy, straight, and rigid rod, about 1 meter long. Side branches and leaves may need to be stripped off a suitable branch, which must be shaped to a sharp tip with the chimpanzees' incisors. This probe is inserted deep into the ground, sometimes needing a grip with feet as well as hands to force it in, then extracted and sniffed. When the scent reveals a nest has been penetrated, the chimpanzee can go on to the next step. For this, a quite different tool is needed: a slender, flexible, but tough probe at least 50 centimeters long, with one end deliberately frayed by pulling over the teeth to make a brush-tip. The chimpanzee now probes with this shorter, flexible tool, into the hole that has previously been made to the underground nest— "fishing" for the termites. Because soldier termites attack the foreign object they detect in their nest, they can be gently withdrawn on the fishing probe and eaten.[12]

This fascinating description of chimpanzee toolmaking illustrates a behavior strikingly similar to that of humans. It goes beyond the merely instinctual behavior that we would expect of an animal and into deliberate planning and execution.

Another interesting, albeit disturbing, behavioral similarity to humans is the chimpanzee's propensity to wage war. Many animals are territorial and will take various measures to mark and protect their territory. For example, I had a very little dog who was apparently delusional about her actual size and would protect the borders of our yard by barking ferociously, lunging, and chasing intruders that, had they not been amused, would have eaten her for a snack. Not only are the chimpanzees clearly smarter than my dog, but they will go beyond defending their territory and aggressively raid other communities in "commando" fashion.[13] They will kill males and young infants and take the females back to their own community. While

11. Byrne, "Dividing Line," 17.
12. Byrne, "Dividing Line," 17–18.
13. Byrne, "Dividing Line," 19.

it may not be pleasant to admit, this behavior is similar to that of humans, although it is different from the peace-loving bonobos.

Like humans, bonobos and chimpanzees recognize themselves in a mirror. This is not a test of general recognition of something in the mirror or a curiosity concerning the creature that the chimpanzee or bonobos sees. What researchers are looking for in the "mirror-recognition test," whether with human infants or with the chimpanzees and bonobos, is whether the reflection is recognized as the "self." This entails researchers looking for a "change from responding with social behavior (reaching out, laughing) to self-directed behavior (interest in the relationship of reflection and their own movements)."[14] It is this type of self-directed recognition that both chimpanzees and bonobos exhibit.[15] Many scientists suggest that this sort of self-recognition indicates a level of self-consciousness similar to humans.[16] Not all agree with this assessment, however; it remains a topic of study.

Two other characteristics that humans are purported to in some way have in common with chimpanzees and bonobos are worth some consideration. The first characteristic is that chimpanzees and bonobos (as well as gorillas) live in community. They have a society. "Like people," de Waal explains, "animals [primates] have friends and enemies, and they certainly do not treat them in the same manner."[17] Within the community, in other words, the nonhuman primates recognize other specific individuals. If you think about a classroom as a community of learners, humans recognize the group as a whole (my class), as well as individuals identified by a name associated with particular physical features (Dr. Vanden Berg, the female teacher at the front of the room). Recognition of other specific individuals can involve some sort of planned interaction with the individual, maybe aggression, comfort, or even reconciliation.[18] In addition, chimpanzees can exhibit either sharing or blatant self-interest when food is presented,[19] much like humans. In short, the bonobos and chimpanzees live in

---

14. Putz, "Moral Apes," 618.

15. Putz, "Moral Apes," 618; De Waal, *Peacemaking among Primates*, 185–87.

16. Both Putz and Byrne argue for the self-consciousness of chimpanzees. Putz also affirms, quoting De Waal, that chimpanzees and bonobos have a theory of the mind. See Putz, "Moral Apes," 619.

17. De Waal, *Peacemaking among Primates*, 38.

18. De Waal, *Peacemaking among Primates*, 42.

19. De Waal, *Good Natured*, 22–23.

community and interact with one another in this community in ways that are remarkably similar to humans.

The second, and somewhat more controversial similarity is the display among these groups of certain moral emotions. Moral emotions are often considered precursors to morality, a topic we will cover a bit later. Three moral emotions we will consider here are empathy, sympathy, and altruism. These emotions are often thought to be something only humans display, but that is likely not the case. For example, Putz reports, "Numerous cases of empathy involving third-order intentionality leading to selfless behavior have been reported in great apes."[20] Third-order intentionality is me wanting you to know that I want you to know something or do something. I want you to know my intentions. This sort of third-order intentionality that Putz identifies with empathy also underlies what De Waal identifies as sympathy, as will be shown below.

Empathy is the ability to understand another person "from his or her frame of reference rather than one's own," which could include "vicariously experiencing that person's feelings, perceptions, and thoughts."[21] Some researchers further distinguish between cognitive empathy, where one "is able to recognize and understand another's mental state," and affective empathy where one "has the ability to share the feelings of others, without any direct emotional stimulation to oneself."[22] In humans, cognitive empathy enables us to imagine ourselves in the place of the other, understand the difficulties of the other, and extrapolate how to react to and interact with the other.[23] For example, De Waal writes,

> To explain how [cognitive empathy] works, imagine that a friend
> has lost both arms in a car accident. Just from seeing his condi-
> tion, or hearing about it, we will grasp the reduction in physical
> ability he has undergone. We can imagine what it is like to have
> no arms, and our capacity for empathy allows us to extrapolate

20. Putz, "Moral Apes," 620. See also De Waal, *Peacemaking among Primates*, 85. De Waal here refers to a 1982 study by Gallup that concluded chimpanzees displayed empathy. However, De Waal, at least in this chapter, seems unconvinced by that data. A bit later in this same book but based on his own observations, he notes that bonobos do appear to act out of empathy, that is, out of an understanding of the other's situation. See p. 195.

21. American Psychological Association, "Empathy."

22. See for example, Kerr-Gafney, Harrison, and Tchanturia, "Cognitive and Affective Empathy."

23. De Waal, *Good Natured*, 48.

this knowledge to the other's situation. Our friend's dog, by contrast, will need time to learn that there is no point in bringing her master a stick to fetch, or that the familiar pat on the back is being replaced by a foot rub. Dogs are smart enough to get used to such changes, but their accommodation is based on learning rather than understanding.[24]

Notice that cognitive empathy only deals with the knowledge of the other's situation, sometimes including their emotional state. Empathy, De Waal suggests, is merely the ability to "recognize someone's pain," something that he points out even a torturer can do.

Sympathy, however, goes beyond empathy. Sympathy is the ability or will to do something about the pain of the other out of concern for the other's well-being.[25] In fact, the main distinction between empathy and sympathy is this motivation or intention to help. De Waal writes that the blurring of this distinction between empathy and sympathy is problematic because "it ignores the distinction between the ability to recognize someone else's pain [empathy] and perhaps their emotional state, and the impulse to do something about it [sympathy]."[26] Sympathy, unlike empathy, includes intention. Because intentions are difficult, if not impossible to determine in animals, De Waal offers an animal equivalent of human sympathy. He calls this "succorant behavior."[27] Succorant behavior is "helping, caregiving, or providing relief to distressed or endangered individuals other than progeny."[28] In his studies of various animal populations, De Waal observes succorant behavior in a variety of animals, including dolphins, whales, elephants, and dogs, as well as the nonhuman primate populations he specializes in. In one example, De Waal describes a diseased whale that beaches itself. This whale is surrounded by twenty-nine healthy whales who stayed with the beached whale for three days until it died.[29] Other examples include special care of handicapped monkeys, reactions of various animals to death of one of their own, and protection of injured individuals, including treatment of their wounds, suggest some level of sympathy exists in a variety of animal

24. De Waal, *Good Natured*, 48.
25. De Waal, *Good Natured*, 66.
26. De Waal, *Good Natured*, 41.
27. De Waal, *Good Natured*, 41.
28. De Waal, *Good Natured*, 41.
29. De Waal, *Good Natured*, 42.

populations.[30] These behaviors in both nonhuman primates and other mammals look much like what humans would identify as sympathy. So at the very least there seems to be some level of similarity with humans here, although De Waal admits that these observations are inconclusive due to the difficulty in ascertaining intent in animals.[31] Indeed, in spite of these observations, De Waal is skeptical that animals display sympathy in part because "human sympathy demands a well-developed sense of self and the ability to assume another individual's perspective,"[32] something that is not clearly true of nonhuman animals.

That leaves the third moral emotion we should consider: altruism. Altruism can be defined as the decision to put someone else's interest beside or above one's own. This behavior is seemingly unselfish, especially in that it often benefits the other at some cost to the one who is acting altruistically. In addition to this generic sort of altruism, de Waal offers a more specific understanding of altruism that moves beyond the sort of cooperative behavior one might observe in a group. He calls this "cognitive altruism." Cognitive altruism takes into account not just the cooperative behavior but also the intention or motivation behind the behavior.[33] De Waal writes, "the precise *intention* behind [the cooperative behavior] changes as soon as the actor can picture what his assistance means to the other." When the perspective of the other is taken into account, it "revolutionizes helpful behavior, turning it into cognitive altruism, that is, altruism with the other's interests explicitly in mind."[34] In other words, altruism moves beyond intent to help, to a recognition and taking account of the other's state of mind. While there may be evidence for some sort of empathy or even sympathy among animals, there is little evidence for the sort of targeted behavior that is associated with altruism. Thus, the similarity between humans and animals in the area of these three moral emotions is very limited with respect to altruistic behavior, if for no other reason than the necessity for communication to establish the intent that is integral to the emotion of altruism.

The survey of how humans are similar to other animals, including the two species that have occupied our thinking above, could continue.

---

30. De Waal, *Good Natured*, 49–51, 53–57, 58. See also De Waal, "Natural Normativity."

31. De Waal, *Good Natured*; for his extended discussion see especially pp. 40–88.

32. De Waal, *Good Natured*, 82.

33. De Waal, *Good Natured*, 83.

34. De Waal, *Good Natured*, 83.

Crows, for example, manufacture hooks from specific materials in order to aid their foraging.[35] Dolphins form social groups and alliances that help protect them from a variety of threats.[36] Whales are known to form strong attachments to each other and will support and help weak members in their pods.[37] Elephants appear to care for and miss their dead.[38] Regardless of the list of similarities between human and animal behavior, even that of our closest evolutionary relatives, these animals are not human. The differences are as substantial as the similarities are interesting. The following section will explore some of those differences and what science is teaching us about human special uniqueness.

Human Physical Dissimilarity from Other Creatures

In discussions of human uniqueness, it is quite common to hear the assertion that our likeness to other animals, particularly our nearest evolutionary relatives, should be seen as a difference in degree, not necessarily in kind.[39] Turning now from our survey of similarities to an examination of some dissimilarities, we will be served well overall if we consider throughout this section whether or at what point the differences in degree might actually constitute a difference in kind, a question we will attempt to answer at the end of this survey. We will begin this section on dissimilarity with observations of physical characteristics. Because of their remarkable similarity to humans, we will pay special attention here, as in the last section, to nonhuman primates, especially to our closest genomic relatives, the chimpanzees and bonobos. We will give an occasional nod to other species of animals when appropriate, however.

The first thing one might notice in observing these creatures is that they are covered with fur, as are most mammals. Modern humans have lost that protective covering as well as the large canine teeth that the chimpanzees and bonobos still have. Nonhuman primates in general have retained these physical features. Another fairly obvious physical characteristic is that the human stance is also different from that of our nonhuman primate

35. Clump, Cantat, and Rutz, "Raw-material Selectivity."

36. MacIntyre, *Dependent, Rational, Animals*, 63.

37. De Waal, *Good Natured*, 41–42.

38. Sefina, "Depths of Animal Grief."

39. See, for example, Moritz, "Human Uniqueness," 65. I have seen this basic phrase attributed to Darwin, but no one seems to cite where exactly Darwin states this.

relatives. Humans are bipedal and upright. That is, we walk upright on two feet. We are, in fact, the only vertebrates that are structured in this way. For example, Francisco Ayala points out that birds, too, are bipedal, "but their backbone is horizontal rather than vertical."[40] The great apes, by contrast, predominantly walk on all four limbs, carrying part of their weight on their arms. At the very least, this upright stance frees human arms and hands for purposes other than locomotion. The ratio of the length between arms and legs is reflective of this difference in purpose. The arms of other primates are proportionally longer than human arms, while their legs are proportionally shorter than human legs.[41] If we turn to faces, a close look at the eyes of humans will show that the part of the eye that surrounds the iris (the sclera) is white. In chimpanzees it is dark. Sweating, too, is a uniquely human function. Most mammals pant to cool off but humans—and only humans—secrete water onto their skin for the purpose of helping them stay cool.[42]

There are also somewhat less obvious physical characteristics that are different in humans than in most other primates. Cryptic ovulation is one such characteristic. While most female animals, including the chimpanzees, have some way of letting males know that they are fertile, human females "show no outward markers of their fertile phase."[43] Related to this, unlike most other primates who remain capable of conception for most of their lives, human females go through menopause rendering them infertile for about a third of their lifespan.[44]

The human genome is another distinctive feature. Humans share somewhere between 98 and 99 percent of their genome with chimpanzees and bonobos, depending on how insertions and deletions are accounted for.[45] What that means is that humans genetically differ from chimpanzees and bonobos by about 42 million base pairs out of a total of about three billion.[46] As a point of reference, the DNA difference between individual humans is about 0.1 percent, or 300,000 base pairs. When one looks at the numbers, the percentage difference between humans and the two

40. Ayala, "Biology Precedes, Culture Transcends," 512.

41. O'Neil, "Humans."

42. Wernick, "Sweating."

43. Suddendorf, *Gap*, 2.

44. O'Neil, "Humans."

45. Fridovich-Keil, "Human Genome."

46. Wolchover, "Chimps vs. Humans."

chimpanzees is quite low, however the actual number of differing base pairs—42 million—is very large, clearly large enough to account for the many unique characteristics of humans that are not shared with other primates.

From a slightly different angle, of the total approximately three billion base pairs in human DNA, 99 percent is noncoding, serving various regulatory functions of DNA copying instead.[47] The other 1 percent of human DNA are genes. Genes are sections of DNA that code for proteins, and most estimates suggest that humans have somewhere between 20,000 and 25,000 genes. Many of these genes are identical to those of chimpanzees but are used differently by the two species. In summary, while the similarities are numerous, the small difference in DNA sequence, as well as the differences in how various genes are actually used, adds up to a range of different physical features, as well as substantial differences in behavior between humans and our most similar living genetic relatives.

Humans also differ from chimpanzees and bonobos in brain size and organization. Human brains are about three times larger than the brains of chimps. But it is not just the size that is the most significant difference. About half of our 170 billion brain cells are neurons, that is, cells whose job it is to transmit various sorts of information. A study by Mora-Bermudez et al. notes that the human cerebral cortex, which supports most of our thinking, contains about two times the number of neurons as that same region in chimpanzees.[48] In addition, they explain that the "networks of brain cells in the cerebral cortex also behave differently in the two species."[49] These differences begin already in development, specifically during cell division. Chimpanzee brain cells tend toward more differentiation, while human brain cells tend toward proliferation. The result is that humans end up with substantially more neurons in the cerebral cortex than chimpanzees.[50] In other words, this difference is genetically, and not environmentally, directed.

The reason the difference in number and function of neurons is so important is because of an even more important difference: the human ability to think and reason. The way humans think and reason is linked to the sort of brain we have, although many of the details of why we are able to think as

47. National Library of Medicine, "What Is Noncoding DNA?"
48. Mora-Bermudez et al., "Differences and Similarities."
49. Mora-Bermudez et al., "Differences and Similarities."
50. Mora-Bermudez et al., "Differences and Similarities."

we do remain unknown. What we do know is that humans, unlike the two chimpanzees, are able to think abstractly in very complex ways that include categorizing, reasoning, and imagination. These, as well as certain other activities, are often described as activities of the mind and are discussed, especially in psychological circles, as theory of mind.

Human Theory of Mind and Metacognition

Theory of mind is, according to Justin L. Barrett and Matthew J. Jarvinen, "cognitive and developmental psychology jargon that refers to the typical way in which a human (or other sophisticated animal) attributes mental states and thinks about the interrelationships and roles of those mental states in directing action (also known as folk psychology)."[51] For example, when I speak to my husband, I am aware that as I am speaking he is listening and already forming thoughts about what I am saying. In addition, I have some notion of what those thoughts might be and how he may respond. And it is not just that we can think about what we think or what someone else might think. "We seem to be able to put ourselves into another's shoes," Suddendorf writes, "and imagine how we would feel or what we would think if we were in their situation."[52] Our minds are wired to the social network around us.[53] We evaluate the state of mind of others, making judgments about what someone might be thinking or planning and adjust our own thoughts and behavior according to what we think is going on.

The ability to attribute mental states to others is unique to humans, for the most part. No other animal demonstrates the capacity for the sort of complex "mind reading" that humans engage in, although as one author points out, it is very difficult to assess this ability in animals that do not have speech.[54] That said, some studies do suggest some capacity for chimpanzees and bonobos to reason at basic levels about other minds. For example, in 2001 Brian Hall, Josep Call, and Michael Tomasello published findings suggesting that "at least in some situations (i.e., competition with conspecifics [i.e., members of the same species]) chimpanzees know what conspecifics have and have not seen (do and do not know), and that they

51. Barrett and Jarvinen, "Cognitive Evolution," 170.
52. Suddendorf, *Gap*, 114.
53. Suddendorf, *Gap*, 115.
54. Suddendorf, *Gap*, 31.

use this information to devise effective social-cognitive strategies."[55] In other words, there is evidence that chimpanzees think about other minds. As Suddendorf writes, "The wealth of recent positive data from the great apes suggest, though they certainly do not prove, that they have limited understanding of basic mental states."[56] The jury is still out, and research continues into the sort of mind reading in which chimpanzees can engage.

Despite the positive evidence for some form of chimpanzee mind reading or metacognition, the degree to which they appear to engage in these behaviors is never beyond that of a human preschool-aged child. In many cases, the ability remains similar to that of a toddler. In addition, while certain great apes may be able to reason about some basic states of mind, they do not seem to care much about connecting with other minds. This connection with other minds, something that even human infants show interest in doing, is part of what forms the foundation for cooperation in tasks, teaching, and learning. In other words, the human desire to connect with other minds for various purposes far outstrips that of even the creatures most similar to us: the great apes. Indeed, it seems as if humans are hardwired for complex social interactions in ways that are unique to them. Suddendorf writes that the results of ongoing research in this area "add to the mounting evidence that humans' urge to link with other minds is unique." He further notes that for now "there is no strong evidence that apes understand the representational character of beliefs. It remains possible that they only reason about observables, rather than about minds."[57]

This does not mean that these animals are not amazing in the abilities they do have compared with other animals. Further studies may reveal more about the ability of chimpanzees to "mind-read" than researchers are at present able to discern. But even if we grant that chimpanzees have some rudimentary mind-reading skills, the differences between those skills and the mind-reading ability of an adult human—or even an older human child—are huge. It is the case that these metacognitive abilities in which humans excel not only set humans apart from these close genetic relatives, but they also lay the framework for other skills not found elsewhere in the animal world.

---

55. Hare, Call, and Tomasello, "Do Chimpanzees Know?," 139. See also, more recently, Krupenye et al., "Great Apes."

56. Suddendorf, *Gap*, 130.

57. Suddendorf, *Gap*, 132.

Human Speech

One of those skills that is linked to theory of mind is language. Over the years there have been attempts to teach chimpanzees to talk. One early and groundbreaking example was Project Nim, led by Columbia University psychology professor Herbert Terrace. Terrace's aim was to find out if a chimpanzee could learn to communicate with humans. In 2008 Terrace described the goal of his study to an interviewer. "Everyone knows," Terrace said, "that words are learned one at a time." But, he continued, "something happens when children begin to combine words and create true language." The question, Terrace said, was "Could Nim do this?"[58]

In 1973, a young chimp named Nim was placed with a family by Terrace and his colleagues. Over the course of three years, Nim was trained to express his demands in American Sign Language. He learned over 123 signs. In an interview with Carla Cantor forty years after the project ended, Terrace offered these reflections: "Nim learned to sign to obtain food, drink, hugs, and other physical rewards. Nim often got the signs right, but that was because his teachers inadvertently prompted him by making appropriate signs a fraction of a second before he did." The researchers concluded that he was not capable of learning language, only of signing to receive a reward. Nim's signing was not spontaneous and, according to Terrace, "He was unable to use words conversationally, let alone form sentences."[59]

Language differs from animal communication in two respects. Terrace writes that language "allows humans to name things and to create new meanings by recombining words. No animal has those abilities."[60] Richard Byrne, although citing a number of more promising studies conducted with apes using a computerized lexigram system of communication rather than sign language, seems to agree. The studies he cites appeared to have more successes, particularly with bonobos, than earlier studies using sign language. Nonetheless, the bonobo's syntax, Byrne writes, "remained minimal (e.g., weak word-order effects), and usage was still largely a matter of comprehension of commands and generation of requests."[61] Byrne also suggests that if there is a line of demarcation between humans and the two species of chimpanzees, something he seems to doubt, that line is

---

58. Adler, "Chimp That Learned."
59. Cantor, "Project Nim Revisited."
60. Cantor, "Project Nim Revisited."
61. Byrne, "Dividing Line," 24.

most likely language.[62] It is the case that while the great apes are able to use gestures to communicate with each other, this communication falls short of complicated language that humans use.

Suddendorf writes that animal communication is considerably more limited than human language. Animal communication is "restricted to a few types of information exchanges, typically to do with reproduction, territory, food, and alarm,"[63] he writes. By contrast, human language is generative and flexible, creating new words and new usages of old words appropriate to new situations. For example, the word "internet" did not exist before sometime in the mid-1960s. As this newfangled electronic globally connected system came into use, it received a name with which, by now, everyone is familiar. Language is symbolic and, according to Suddendorf, "requires a mind that wants to understand and be understood."[64] In fact, "Language works because individuals agree on the meaning of a set of symbols and how they should be used."[65] In other words, language requires an ability to think about what others are thinking as well as a desire to communicate to others what you are thinking about. That is, language requires a highly developed ability to mind-read. This is what humans do. And we do it almost without realizing it.

Humans are programmed, if you will, to learn and communicate via language. The language-learning platform is inherent in humans. Suddendorf points to a child's language acquisition as proof. "Children acquire language rules effortlessly and without explicit instruction."[66] In fact, as long as the language platform functions properly, humans are able to learn not only whatever language they are born into, but many other languages as well. For example, I have a friend who was born and raised in Korea. Korean is his native language. But my friend is also fluent in English, Dutch, and German as well as having the ability to read and translate Koine Greek, Biblical Hebrew, and Latin. Humans are not just able to learn to speak and communicate in one language, but we are able to cross cultures and learn to communicate just as well in multiple languages. In addition, if the non-native language is learned early enough, it will often be spoken without an accent.

62. Byrne, "Dividing Line," 24.
63. Suddendorf, *Gap*, 81.
64. Suddendorf, *Gap*, 76.
65. Suddendorf, *Gap*, 65.
66. Suddendorf, *Gap*, 73.

In addition to the ability to learn multiple languages, humans can also combine words in a wide variety of ways to explain and describe literally thousands of concepts. Humans both teach and learn from one another in multiple ways but perhaps especially through language, even though language itself is more caught than taught. This desire to teach and learn begins very early. My grandson, when he was still a toddler, never took anything I said at face value. His first question—whether we were reading a book together, playing a game, or cooking—was "oh . . . but why?" (It generally sounded more like one word, however: *oh-bu-why*.) He wanted to understand what we were doing, which he thought I must know given our activity. But he was equally eager to let me know about what he was doing at any given time. I would arrive at his house, and he would run up and say, "Grammy, come over here and let me show you what I am building." The "show you" would inevitably come with a lot of explanation as well. This sort of interaction is also unique to humans. The great apes, by contrast, "do not regularly teach each other, point out things for others' benefit, or ask for the names of things," writes Suddendorf.[67] Byrne notes that, even in the lexigram studies, "doubt remained as to whether any of the subjects really appreciated that they were communicating, in the sense of exchanging ideas with another mind, rather than simply solving artificial puzzles in order to gain reward or comfort."[68] Ongoing research in the area of communication and language may eventually open new understandings about whether or not other animals are capable of the sort of communication that humans take for granted. Unlike humans, animals at this point in evolutionary history appear to care very little about what their same-species peers think beyond some very rudimentary information. This combined lack of interest and inability to build a complex language system minimizes their ability to engage in many other activities that are part and parcel of being human.

Human Morality

One such activity that has often been the subject of study is morality. The first question when dealing with morality is exactly what we mean by the term. Very simply, morality has to do with questions of right and wrong, that which is permissible or impermissible. This entails making value

67. Suddendorf, *Gap*, 86.
68. Byrne, "Dividing Line," 25–26.

judgments about particular behaviors, that is, judging which behaviors are good or beneficial and which are bad or in some way detrimental to oneself or others. Ayala notes that moral judgments are "dictated not by one's own interest or profit but by regard for others, which may cause benefits to particular individuals (altruism) or take into consideration the interests of a social group to which one belongs."[69] When discussing the biological roots of morality, it is helpful to distinguish between these basic value judgments and the accepted norms for what may constitute right and wrong in any given community.[70] In other words, one can have certain instincts that allow one to make judgments about right or wrong apart from a communally accepted system. Communal agreement on a particular moral system is a further development.

One way to consider morality in animals is to examine behaviors that could be considered as *precursors* to morality. Three behaviors, discussed earlier, have been helpful for understanding whether animals exhibit moral behavior: empathy, sympathy, and altruism. As already noted, there is a preponderance of evidence that animals, perhaps especially the chimpanzees, exhibit at least some form of empathy and sympathy, and perhaps even altruism. The question is how do these behaviors compare to fully developed human morality? Ayala thinks there are three conditions that are necessary and "jointly sufficient" for truly moral behavior. The first condition he identifies is "the ability to anticipate the consequences of one's own actions." The second is "the ability to make value judgments," that is, the ability to evaluate the benefit of a potential action to another individual or group. The third condition is the ability "to choose between alternative courses of action."[71] While the first condition could fall under the rubric of adaptive learning, the second condition requires a certain amount of abstract thought, including the ability to think about how the other, including another group, will be affected. In other words, the second condition requires at least an elementary form of theory of mind. The idea that all three conditions are both necessary and jointly sufficient suggests that full-orbed moral behavior requires a level of abstract thought that is beyond the capacity of even the chimpanzees and that is, in fact, uniquely human.[72]

69. Ayala, "Biology Precedes, Culture Transcends," 519.

70. Ayala, "Biology Precedes, Culture Transcends," 516.

71. Ayala, "Biology Precedes, Culture Transcends," 519.

72. Ayala, "Biology Precedes, Culture Transcends," 517.

Oliver Putz, in an essay dealing with animal morality, focuses on the question of whether animals have "the cognitive and affective capacities that enable moral decisions."[73] While Putz does not specify these capacities with the same level of detail as Ayala, he does offer what he calls a psychological benchmark when assessing animal morality. He argues that this benchmark is "neither prosocial behavior nor fairness in a tit-for-tat reciprocity but rather the ability to reflect upon one's choices and their consequences."[74] What is key, for Putz, is possession of some sort of ability to think abstractly about choices. Specifically, Putz thinks that one must possess a theory of mind that allows for "the fissure of the self into the reflecting subject and reflected object."[75] He thinks that apes not only have this ability but have it at a high enough level for us to consider them as truly moral agents.[76]

Suddendorf offers a somewhat different, more hierarchical grid for assessing behaviors as moral or not. Drawing on De Waal, Suddendorf offers three levels of behavior that form the psychological foundation of morality. First is what he calls the "basic building blocks of empathy and reciprocity." The next level includes "the group pressures that keep individuals in line." The third and highest level is "the capacity for self-reflective and moral reasoning and judgment."[77] Level one, as already argued, doesn't require an ability to know or understand what is going on in the mind of another. Level two could fall into the category of adaptive learning or the category of cooperative behaviors. For example, it is well attested that animals exhibit reciprocal behavior, the "I scratch your back, you scratch mine" sorts of cooperation. But Suddendorf points out that these behaviors are "mostly based on kinship rather than on complex and vulnerable systems of reciprocity and reputation" that we see in humans.[78]

When we turn to level three—self-reflection combined with moral reasoning—we move to more abstract thinking and analysis, a rudimentary theory of mind. We humans regulate our own behavior based on our moral assessments of a situation, not just on social pressures or reciprocity. Humans are able to reflect on why we do what we do or why we want what

73. Putz, "Moral Apes," 615.
74. Putz, "Moral Apes," 616.
75. Putz, "Moral Apes," 616.
76. Putz, "Moral Apes," 617–19.
77. Suddendorf, *Gap*, 187.
78. Suddendorf, *Gap*, 191–92.

we want, and change our course as the result of those reflections. Depending on the situation, humans are able to do this in an instant, or deliberate over some period of time. We humans are guided not just by our reason, but also by our emotions, perhaps especially our moral emotions.

According to De Waal, emotions can be divided into two types. "Typical emotions," he writes, "concern only our personal interests—how we have been treated or how we want to be treated—whereas moral emotions go beyond this."[79] Moral emotions are more abstract. They allow speculation on the impact of behavior on the wider community. De Waal writes "It is only when we make judgments of how *anyone* under the circumstances ought to be treated that we speak of moral judgment."[80] While chimpanzees may demonstrate what De Waal calls "community concern," he notes that these behaviors are "a far cry from the human preoccupation with community standards and the welfare of the whole."[81] It is also the case that our primate relatives do not seem to have any sense of obligation beyond their immediate context. Other primates, writes De Waal, "appear unworried about social relationships or situations that they do not directly participate in. They also may not, like humans, feel any obligation to be good, or to experience guilt and shame whenever they fail."[82]

The research on animal morality is ongoing and there remains considerable disagreement among scholars both about how to assess the behaviors they observe in various animals, and whether comparisons to human morality are even legitimate. What is clear is that the behavior observed in animals—including the two species of chimpanzees genetically similar to humans—is not identical to that in humans. While there is evidence, for example, of what we could call altruistic behavior, it does not appear that this behavior is demanded of the group as a whole. Indeed, adherence to an ideal or standard is "only rarely observed . . . in primates at the communal level."[83] Do we observe "Mother Teresa" sort of behavior in other species? I would argue that we do not. We may get occasional glimpses of self-sacrificing behavior, some situational instances, but so far as I can ascertain from the literature, we do not see the sort of ongoing virtuous behavior that

79. De Waal, "Natural Normativity," 198.

80. De Waal, "Natural Normativity," 198.

81. De Waal, "Natural Normativity," 200.

82. De Waal, "Natural Normativity," 200.

83. De Waal, "Natural Normativity," 198.

is observable and generally lauded in humans.[84] Is this a question of degree versus kind? For now, I will leave that question open until we are able to look at the whole picture.

Human Culture-Making

While there are many more aspects of human behavior that we could explore, the last feature of humans we will examine is culture. Ayala asserts that no other animals have a distinct culture. By this he means that animals do not have institutions, codified rules for behavior, or, as he puts it, "all the creations of the human mind."[85] He makes a distinction between biological and cultural inheritance. Biological inheritance is exactly what you expect: the passing along of traits through the genome. The traits that are best suited for continued reproduction and survival will be the most likely to be passed along. Adaptation to changes in the environment generally takes many generations and thousands of years. Not so with cultural inheritance, claims Ayala.

While biological inheritance is important, Ayala thinks that the predominant way that humans have evolved and adapted in history is via cultural inheritance. He writes,

> Cultural inheritance makes possible for people what no other organism can accomplish—the cumulative transmission of experience from generation to generation. Animals can learn from experience, but they do not transmit their experiences, their discoveries (at least not to any large extent), to the following generations. Animals have individual memory, but they do not have a social memory. Humans, on the other hand, have developed a culture because they can transmit their experiences cumulatively from generation to generation.[86]

84. Mother Teresa is an easy example, but there are many others who exhibit this sort of behavior more sporadically. For example, many people acted heroically during World War II by hiding Jews during the Nazi occupation. More recently, firefighters running into the World Trade Center on September 11 could be another example. More day-to-day examples might include stopping to help a stranger with a flat tire, volunteering to help re-build an area hit by a devastating storm, bringing a meal to someone in need, or offering to drive someone to a doctor's appointment.

85. Ayala, "Biology Precedes, Culture Transcends," 513.

86. Ayala, "Biology Precedes, Culture Transcends," 514.

Cultural inheritance in not dependent on DNA. Rather, it is dependent on teaching and learning, whether directly or by example.[87] Unlike biological inheritance, cultural inheritance can change swiftly, even within one generation. Two examples of this phenomenon that he calls cultural evolution are shelter and clothing. While most animals have to adapt to a changing environment over long stretches of time via biological changes in their genome, humans are able to move around to different environments or adapt to an environment through their development of things like clothing and shelter.[88] In addition, "a new scientific discovery or technical achievement can be transmitted to the whole of mankind, potentially at least, in less than one generation."[89] In other words, humans have the ability to change a variety of factors that influence their survival virtually overnight. Ayala optimistically explains, "whenever a need arises, culture can directly pursue the appropriate changes to meet the challenge."

One additional current example of cultural inheritance is apparent in the reaction to the Covid-19 virus. In late 2019, the world became aware of a novel coronavirus that was spreading rapidly near Wuhan, China. Within months, this deadly virus had spread around the world, wreaking havoc on the human population. While it seemed to cause much more death to certain vulnerable populations, the rapidly rising death toll during the first half of 2020 caused alarm and led to a global shutdown of nearly every institution with wide-ranging impact on social structures. By mid-2021, more than 4.13 million persons have died from Covid-19, but the rate of deaths then began to fall. Why? By the end of 2020 scientists had developed a vaccine that prevented either infection or, if infected, the most severe symptoms of the infection. In other words, rather than counting on natural immunity of some who could then pass that immunity on to others via reproduction, humans bypassed this natural evolutionary path, offering immunity to this deadly virus to many. By contrast to this sort of human ingenuity, "biological adaptation depends on the accidental availability of a favorable mutation, or of a combination of several mutations, at the time and place where the need arises."[90] Whether humans are always successful in their endeavors to meet the challenge, as apparently the case with Covid-19, however, is another story.

87. Ayala, "Biology Precedes, Culture Transcends," 513–14.
88. Ayala, "Biology Precedes, Culture Transcends," 514.
89. Ayala, "Biology Precedes, Culture Transcends," 515.
90. Ayala, "Biology Precedes, Culture Transcends," 515.

Of course, some human cultural adaptations arguably decrease survivability and cause harm. Drugs that humans create to treat a condition sometimes turn out to have terrible effects. For example, thalidomide, marketed in the mid-twentieth century as a drug that could alleviate morning sickness turned out to be the cause of devastating birth defects. But Ayala is correct that there is a sense in which humans control their destiny in a way that no other creature (that we know of) can. And this is even more true today than it was in the past. With the sequencing of the human genome and the advent of CRISPR technology for gene editing, humans are able to manipulate their own genome and therefore create adaptations that nature may (or may not) have made but almost certainly would not have made as quickly.[91]

Often discussions about culture turn to questions of cave art or music or some such thing. But Ayala is pointing out something much more basic than merely the ability to produce art or tools. Certainly, tools can help a creature manipulate their environment to their own advantage. But the ability to make a few tools cannot compare to the multitude of ways that humans have found to adapt for necessity, but also for pure pleasure. The reason for this is the extraordinary nature of the human mind. Indeed, the list of things humans can do is amazing. Humans do not have wings, yet we have discovered a variety of ways to fly. We are not built like cheetahs, yet we can outpace them in nearly every modern automobile and for much longer distances. We cannot reach the tops of trees like giraffes, yet we have built bucket trucks and cranes that can reach much higher than any giraffe. We do not have gills, yet we have found ways to swim or dive underwater for long periods of time. We do not have fur like a polar bear, yet, along the lines that Ayala points out, we are able to clothe ourselves and provide shelter for ourselves so that we can live in nearly any climate.[92]

Lest we begin to think too highly of ourselves, this same powerful mind that allows for a multitude of ways to adapt and enhance our lives and the world around us also allows for great harm. Humans have devastated the environment with our lust for more and more consumer goods that are far from necessary. Humans continue to engage in activities that lead to climate change, something that affects the lives of everything on earth. Humans have invented and used weapons of mass destruction that can wipe out millions of living beings in seconds and leave the earth uninhabitable

91. See, for example, Max, "Beyond Human."
92. These ideas build on the basic ideas Ayala points out.

for decades or more. Humans are currently enthralled with technologies that promote social media use, something that is involved in troublesome consequences such as the astronomic rise in suicide rates among teen girls, manipulation of the news we hear, and election interference.[93] Human intelligence, in other words, is just as likely to cause the downfall of societies as to help societies survive. Animals, including the great apes, do not seem to engage in behaviors that will destroy their species, despite the conflicts that sometimes occur between groups.

Difference in Degree vs. Kind?

What is clear from science is that humans (*Homo sapiens*) are very different from even their closest living relatives. Is this difference one of degree and not kind, as so many claim? That is very difficult to ascertain, in part because it is a judgment laced with subjective value and not easily quantifiable. One way to consider this question is through a different lens. When my children were little, one of their favorite books was Richard Scarry's *Cars and Trucks and Things That Go*. The title implies that the overarching category is "things that go." With a category so broad, it may be easy to say that all things considered in that book are of the same kind: "things that go." Indeed, everything in the book possesses a certain similarity with everything else, so do these "things that go" differ only in degree?

If one considers all the "things that go" in the book, however, there are some that are clearly different in kind. For example, there are bikes with no motors, a baby carriage, and a pedal boat along with any number of motorized vehicles. So, what if we narrow the category to "things that go that are motorized." We can see similarities between cars, trucks, and motorcycles in this scenario, but what about boats? So maybe we need to limit the category to "wheeled vehicles with motors." Here we will find a lot of similarity. Every vehicle has wheels, at least two, and some sort of internal combustion engine. But could one say that a motorcycle differs only in degree and not in kind from, say, a car? Or what about a car and a bulldozer? Both have wheels, an internal combustion engine, a drive train, a seat, and a steering

93. For more on this see the Center for Humane Technology (https://www.humane-tech.com), an organization founded by former tech engineers that now counts among its ranks former presidents and CEOs of the tech industry. Their goal is to press for legislation that will reign in the unbridled power of big tech and help users of social media recognize that social media is not the product, but rather the consumer is the product, and the grave ramifications from this shift in the market.

mechanism. Both can get you from point A to point B. Mechanically, they are more alike than different. But do they differ only in degree, or, at some point, as one moves from a car or even a small truck to a bulldozer, are we dealing with a difference in kind?

The difference in degree versus kind question remains fraught with ambiguity, even when the category is narrowed to a point where the things in question have many overlaps. If we go back to the car-bulldozer question, it looks like a good deal of what differentiates these two vehicles is not so much the differences in their structure, although that is not insignificant, but what purpose they were designed to have. While purpose is nearly impossible to surmise where animals (and most creatures) are concerned, it seems clear that numerous similarities between two items, whether they are creatures or things, is a necessary but insufficient condition for claiming that the items in question differ only in degree or that they actually differ in kind. In other words, the degree versus kind question requires additional information. I would suggest that the additional information needed is an assessment of the purpose of the things in question. The question of purpose, however, at least where animals are concerned, moves us out of the realm of empirical science. At least in this section, then, this question will need to remain unanswered.

One group of creatures that we have not engaged in our thinking are the extinct hominin species more closely related to modern humans than are the chimpanzees. Perhaps here, if not with the chimpanzees, there is evidence of humans differing in degree but not kind. After all, modern humans are likely even more closely related to the various extinct hominins than to the chimpanzees. The problem with examining behaviors in human ancestors that are no longer living is that, to a higher degree than even with apes, we cannot talk to them. Indeed, we cannot observe them at all. This does not mean that we know nothing about them. There is evidence of the sorts of things various groups were capable of doing—making tools, some burial rituals, art, and so on—but many of the activities that it appears these human precursors did were not much different from what we observe in the chimpanzees. Some researchers assume parsimony between early hominins and chimpanzees to help figure out what sorts of behaviors one might expect in the hominins.[94] This seems like a good method, but

---

94. For an excellent, if a bit dated, article on how researchers work through the remains of these hominins and their groups to come to conclusions about their behaviors see Stearley, "Assessing Evidences."

it doesn't get us much closer to understanding how ancient hominins and modern humans are alike than current research into chimpanzee behavior, at least from the standpoint of a nonspecialist like myself. So we end up back at the question whether humans diverge only in degree but not kind from earlier hominins, a question to which the answer is not terribly clear.

What this chapter does show is that other animals and humans are remarkably similar, something that is undoubtedly true about humans and ancient hominins as well. But the chapter also shows that the differences between humans and other animals are even more remarkable, something that may or may not be true of a comparison between modern humans and other hominins. What is peculiar where hominins are concerned is that, unlike any other species, of all the other hominins that have been found, humans are the only one that survived. Ian Tattersall explains:

> The notion of one unique, gradually perfecting human lineage fits well with the undeniable fact that there is only one hominid species in the world today: a single entity that we are tempted to project back into the past, to produce a chain of ancestors becoming steadily less like us as they recede into the mists of time. But analysis of the hominid fossil record, which has vastly expanded over the past few decades, shows very clearly that this was not the pattern at all. At virtually all points in human evolutionary history, several hominid species have coexisted (and at least intermittently competed). That *Homo sapiens* is the lone hominid [sic] in the world today is a highly atypical situation.[95]

Given all the hominins that we know of, it is indeed peculiar that only this species (*Homo sapiens*) survived, perhaps especially if we consider that some of the other hominins may have been intellectually fairly similar to modern humans.[96] It is clear from the fossil record that modern humans displaced other hominins wherever they went. The intriguing question, then, is "Why?" The answer to that question, at least for now, remains elusive.

95. Tattersall, *Paleontology*, 151. It is my understanding that the proper term Tattersall should have used is *hominin*, not *hominid*, since there are at least eight hominid species alive today. Thank you to Dr. Ryan Bebej for pointing this out.

96. Stearley, "Assessing Evidences," 168.

Conclusion

Given the intellectual capacity of modern humans, it is safe to say that humans are more capable than any other animal of both great evil and great good. Perhaps therein lies some of the reason for the disappearance of other hominins. Indeed, humans don't just do great good and evil, but they are able to plan and execute good and evil. They know the consequences of their actions on what is around them, including the impact on the nonsentient world, and they are able to adjust their actions to suit their intended goals, and often quite successfully. No animal has the unique intellectual capacities that humans have, regardless of whether one judges this to be a difference in degree or kind. Humans are physically similar to the two types of chimpanzees, as well as the now nonexistent hominins, right down to our DNA, yet the differences are striking. Behaviorally, humans and other animals share many interesting characteristics, from sociability to theory of mind. Nonetheless, these similarities begin to pale when one considers the differences. Perhaps the most profound difference, as noted above, is the human ability to mold, shape, and transmit culture—literally to shape their world and their destiny. No other animal has that capability. The effects of human ability to shape their destiny places them in a category of their own. From a scientific perspective, then, it is fair to say that humans are specially unique. What this might mean when combined with what we know from Scripture and theology is the subject of the next chapter.

4

To Harmonize or Not to Harmonize

By now, we have considered human special uniqueness from the perspective of Thomas Aquinas, Scripture, and science. Both Aquinas, whose work is deeply dependent on Scripture, and Scripture itself offer portrayals of humans as specially unique. In the last chapter we introduced evidence from the physical world as understood by various scientists whose observations are both supported by and support the theory of evolution. Although our evidence was inconclusive as to whether science demonstrates humans as unique only in degree or also in kind, it is the case that one of the biggest challenges to the idea of humans as specially unique comes from science, evolutionary science in particular.

The theory of evolution seems to challenge traditional Christian notions of humans as unique beings with unique dignity at least in part because of the claim that humans are not specially created by God, but rather came into being gradually, over a long period of time, descending from other creatures. These sorts of challenges cause anxiety for many Christians who understand Scripture as the primary authority for faith and life. In particular, many Christians worry that the idea of human persons evolving from other forms of life undermines both the biblical creation account that portrays humans as a special creation of God and the basic human dignity that all humans are purported to have according to the Christian tradition. These are weighty concerns and deserve to be taken seriously.

My concern in this chapter, therefore, is primarily pastoral. On the one hand, many scientists have felt both disrespected by Christians who refuse to take some of their findings seriously and offended by those who suggest that science is at "war" with biblical teaching, actively trying to undermine faith. This kind of fear or skepticism toward the work of science undermines explanations of the physical world that underpin everything from medicine to rocket science. It also depicts an uncharitable picture of scientists whose faith is at times called into question because of their findings.

On the other hand, many Christians who are not scientists find themselves in something of a pre-Reformation position with respect to Scripture, being told either directly or indirectly that their straightforward reading of the biblical text cannot be trusted, that they need the academic experts in Old and New Testament to tell them what any given text really means. They cannot discern a reliable meaning of the text at any level on their own. This causes a fair amount of distress to the ordinary Christians who sit in our churches, participate in Bible studies, and engage Scripture as a central part of their piety. In addition, many in the non-Western church take supernatural activity and God's intervention in the world as a given.[1] While they may not be hostile to science, neither do they see the need to harmonize a straightforward reading of the biblical text, including texts like Genesis 1–2, with the findings of modern science, as is quite common in Western theology. Indeed, in the West, when the story of science and that of Scripture collide, it is not unusual for the biblical text to be reinterpreted in order to make the two fit neatly together.[2]

To address this pastoral challenge, this chapter will consider how to think about the relationship between science and Scripture and, by inference, theology due to its dependence on Scripture. I will suggest that we read science and Scripture as two stories that overlap at points, but that also have differences so significant that various attempts at harmonization could undermine the integrity of both stories. I will begin by simply offering a comprehensive summary of evolution, what the concept does teach

1. See, for example, Tennant, *Theology in the Context*, 178–80. For more on the non-Western church, see Jenkins, *New Faces of Christianity*. In addition to these two fine works, my own experience teaching and advising international students at Calvin Seminary has been formative. These very sophisticated students, some with backgrounds in science, seem surprised at Western theology's insistence that Genesis 1 is *not* referring to six days, most often twenty-four-hour days. Care must be taken in these discussions, as well as more recent discussions dealing with sexuality, that the Western church does not impose a new colonialism on the non-Western church. Rather, the Western church must assume a posture of listening to the Spirit's voice in our non-Western brothers and sisters.

2. This is probably most common with Genesis 1–2 and the way we understand the history of life on earth, but it is becoming more common in other areas where science and Scripture also may disagree.

and what it does not—or in some cases *cannot*—teach. My hope is that this explanation will help Christians who are fearful of science recognize and appreciate the good work that scientists accomplish. I will then consider the gap between what we can know about humans from science and what we can know about humans from Scripture, considering especially the issues that arise when we push for harmonization of the two sources. I will then suggest that rather than harmonization, we should retrieve the very Christian idea of *paradox*, recognizing both science and Scripture as two stories that could be held in tension, affirming both the good work of scientific discovery *and* the authority of Scripture as our guide for faith and life. To further elucidate this idea, I will retrieve Aquinas's understanding of the relationship of revealed truths and other types of knowledge, an understanding that recognizes the value of reason, but the priority of Scripture.

The Science of Evolution

One place to begin this brief explanation of evolution is with the notion of "theory." It is not particularly uncommon, whether one is dealing with a secular person or Christian skeptic of evolution, to hear the objection that after all, evolution is *only* a theory. This sort of assertion is both unhelpful and misleading. Unfortunately, in everyday language the word "theory" is often used to refer to something like a hunch with little evidential support. So perhaps my grandson has been misbehaving lately. Because I live some distance away and do not see him often, in a conversation with his mother I tell her I have a theory about his behavior. I suggest that since he has just started school and is no longer at home or with his daycare provider but in a large class, he needs more attention and is striving to receive that attention in a bad way. While it is true that sometimes children behave badly to receive attention, I have no evidence that this is the case with my grandson. It is pure speculation—a speculation that I have labeled as a theory. Thus, the common parlance that some proposition or other is *only* a theory arises not from the scientific use of that term, but from a more colloquial form.

But this is not how the word "theory" is used scientifically. From a scientific perspective, a theory is more like a broad explanation for a wide range of phenomena. The *Oxford English Dictionary* offers this definition of "theory": "an explanation of phenomena arrived at through examination and contemplation of the relevant facts; a statement of one or more laws or principles which are generally held as describing an essential property of something."[3] In other words, a theory is not mere speculation. It is based on conclusions drawn from evidence of some phenomenon via observation, examination, and, in the case of science, experimentation. Insofar as the method is sound, the conclusions are reliable.

Furthermore, in order for an idea to be accepted as a theory by the scientific community, a theory must be strongly supported not only by a single source of evidence but by many different lines of evidence. Evolution is just such a theory. It is so well supported by many lines of evidence from a broad range of scientific disciplines that it is closer to being a fact, similar to the theory of gravity. The question is no longer whether there is evolution, but how best to understand evolution. While scientific theories are always subject to testing and evaluation due to new evidence and therefore subject to new nuance and change, it is highly unlikely that a settled theory like evolution would be overturned. As biologist John Brubacher put it, "I cannot make sense of biology without evolutionary theory, any more than a chemist can make it through the day without atomic theory."[4] What Brubacher is affirming is that the theory of evolution works. It helps make sense of the evidence and offers potential for further theorizing about life and how life develops. Evolution is a good working model—at this point in time the *best* working model—of the development of life on earth. From a Christian perspective, then, evolution could be understood as a scientific description, based on physical evidence, of how God created life on earth.

At the heart of evolution is the idea of descent with modification. This idea suggests that all living things are related to one another through common ancestry. There is evidence for common ancestry in, for example, the fossil record, the genetic record, and in homology, which is the comparison of various physical structures between species. Descent with modification refers specifically to the genome, the biochemical coding that tells cells what to do. A gene is a piece of DNA. Denis Alexander describes the genetic code as "extremely elegant."[5] He explains that "there are four 'letters' in the DNA. . . . Each 'genetic word' composed of three letters is known as a codon."[6] These genes or "genetic words" encode for amino acids, which are the building blocks of proteins. Proteins, writes, Alexander, "carry out most

---

3. *Oxford English Dictionary*, s.v. "theory."

4. Brubacher, "Not Just Another Animal," 23.

5. Denis Alexander, *Is There Purpose?* 106.

6. Alexander, *Is There Purpose?* 106.

of the essential functions of our bodies that keep us alive."[7] In addition, genes are part of chromosomes and are replicable. Richard Dawkins writes, "Genes . . . can self-copy for ten million generations and scarcely degrade at all."[8] Evolution only occurs when there is a change in gene frequency within a population over time. These genetic differences are heritable and can be passed on to the next generation—which is what really matters in evolution: long-term change and survival of the species.

So what might this look like, and what might cause such changes? One example of evolution in action is the story of the peppered moths in England. Peppered moths exist in two varieties: a lighter slightly speckled variety and a dark variety. During the industrial revolution in the nineteenth century, pollution levels were high in various areas of the country. In these areas soot covered everything from buildings to trees. Over time, these industrial areas saw a decrease in the population of the light-colored moths and an increase in the dark-colored moths. Why? In short, because the dark-colored moths had an advantage over their lighter cousins. Their coloring was better suited to the environment. The soot allowed them to more easily blend into their surroundings protecting them from predators, birds that found them to be a tasty meal. Conversely, the light-colored moths could no longer camouflage because of the black soot that covered many of the typical places where moths would rest. They became easy targets for the birds. And, of course, the more dark-colored moths that survive, the more those moths are able to replicate, thus increasing the number of dark-colored genes in the pool of peppered moths. In this case, environmental pressure changed the population density of both types of moths, preferencing one over the other based on survivability.[9]

Daniel Dennett describes the role of biological advantage well. He suggests that we think about a group of organisms well-adapted to a particular environment. They reproduce over and over again until, at some point, the resources that support them begin to run out. The lack of resources prevents some of the population from surviving at all. In addition, some will be unable to produce children. Species that survive will overpopulate with only the most well-adapted individuals surviving. In some cases, the surviving individual may just be lucky, but in many, perhaps even most,

7. Alexander, *Is There Purpose?* 106.

8. Dawkins, *River Out of Eden*, 19.

9. For a more recent study that confirmed the findings of earlier studies on this topic see Cook et al., "Selective Bird Predation."

cases, it will have a genetic advantage. This is at the heart of what is called "natural selection."[10]

In the case of the moths, the population of the dark-colored variety increases, and therefore more genes for dark-colored moths enter the population, tilting the peppered moth population in the direction of dark-colored moths and opening the door for the extinction of light-colored moths. So, the peppered moths offer observation of a population adapting and changing. But what about the development of a whole new species? How can evolution account for speciation, the gradual change from one species into another? In addition to environmental pressures that select or favor one group over another, populations can also change via gene mutation. A mutation is a change in the DNA or genetic code of some particular organism. Usually mutations are small and can be quite insignificant or even detrimental. But sometimes mutations give rise to some variation that gives a particular group an advantage. The accumulation of small mutations over time are part of what can lead to larger variations within a population and, eventually, speciation.[11] In addition, genes and their effects are not considered only in isolation but in interaction with their environment.[12] Insofar as a gene in interaction with the environment, including other genes, will enhance one's chances to survive long enough to reproduce, that particular gene and the trait it specifies for will likely continue. Over a very long period of time—millions of years, in fact—accumulated enhancements may change an organism enough so that it is no longer able to reproduce with the organism it originated from. It is now a divergent species.

On divergence into various species, Dennett notes that tiny variations, from generation to generation, can lead to large differences in phenotype, that is, physiological characteristics. Writing about Darwin and natural selection he notes, "Natural selection would inevitably produce *adaptation* . . . and under the right circumstances, [Darwin] argued, accumulated adaptation would create speciation."[13] Alister McGrath helpfully summarizes this idea at the genetic level in his evaluation of Dawkins's idea of selfish genes. "Successful genes," McGrath writes, "are those that cause phenotypic effects

---

10. Dennett, *Darwin's Dangerous Idea*, 40–42.

11. For a wonderful description of how mutations work and the changes they can make in a population over time, including increasing complexity, see Alexander, *Is There Purpose?* 58–103.

12. Dawkins, *River Out of Eden*, 27.

13. Dennett, *Darwin's Dangerous Idea*, 43.

which promote their survival."[14] Unfortunately, most simple depictions of evolution are misleading because of their simplicity.

The popular museum picture of a chimpanzee that gradually becomes larger and more upright until it becomes human is an unfortunate example of this and leads to the question some people have about whether they descended from an ape. Another simplistic picture that still appears in resources is the tree of life with an organism at the bottom that branches to an ape, one of whose sub-branches eventually leads to a human. While this is slightly better than the common museum depiction of a chimpanzee growing into human, it is only *slightly* better. In reality, one should think of any sort of tree of life as having some nondescript organism at the bottom that eventually divides into a branch, one arm of which becomes a modern primate, and one arm of which becomes a human. In addition, there is more and more evidence that this branching is not only vertical, but horizontal as well.[15] Overall, we are, from an evolutionary standpoint, more like cousins who share a common ancestor than great-great-grandparent and child when it comes to our relationship with modern primates.

This brief introduction to the evolutionary platform from which modern biological science works is intended to help clarify what scientists understand about the history of life on earth and the basic premises from which modern science operates. While it has not yet been mentioned directly, the theory of evolution implies that the earth is very old, something affirmed not only by biologists, but by geologists, chemists, and astronomers as well. Because of the length of time necessary for evolution to occur, the data supporting an old earth fits well with the data that supports evolution. Through the lens of evolution, scientists can offer insights into where humans fit in the world. Specifically, scientists are well-equipped to help us see through their specialized lens how humans are physically both like and unlike the rest of creation, something we considered in the last chapter.

The Science-Scripture Gap

The description of humans that scientists offer is not without problems however. One of the more difficult problems is trying to figure out the

14. McGrath, *Dawkins' God*, 43.

15. McGrath, *Dawkins' God*, 54. McGrath here footnotes several scientific articles that are helpful with respect to understanding horizontal branching. Interested readers should look into these references.

relationship between the scientific evidence regarding human persons and the witness of the biblical text. Of course this is not a new problem. Theologians and scientists who are Christians have been working out different ways to make sense of what could be called the two stories for many years. The results of this thinking can be considered along something of a spectrum. At one end are the young earth creationists. At the other are the various forms of theistic evolution. In between lies everything from old earth creation to intelligent design to evolutionary creation with many variations and overlaps throughout.

While some of these theories claim to be non-harmonizing, most attempt, at least in some measure, to bring together scientific and biblical accounts of the world, particularly in the areas of the age of the earth and the development of life. While at first blush this seems reasonable, these attempts invariably end up either giving preference to the biblical story at the expense of the scientific one, or to the scientific story at the expense of the biblical one. None that I know of are fully balanced. Many of these harmonizing models affirm in some form the idea of the authoritative nature of all of Scripture. But some of the models that affirm biblical authority add so many layers to the interpretation of the biblical text that the average person sitting in the pew has no hope of understanding the purported "true meaning" of the text. On the other side of the science/Bible coin, some models that heartily affirm the authority of Scripture reject in part or in full the findings of modern science. These models tend to rely on a woodenly literal reading of Scripture that takes little account of grammar, literary genre, or historical context, let alone the history of exegesis of the text in the church. In other words, regardless of which story one tends to side with, most accounts leave readers on the other side unsatisfied, as is evidenced by the ongoing debates between the various groups.

Fairly common among the models overall are objections like this one: "Scripture is not intended as a moral guide book or a collection of propositions to believe. Its purpose is to reveal God's plan and purposes throughout human history."[16] These general objections, however, are hardly helpful for trying to make sense of what we read, particularly when we get down to the details of the story. Of course the Bible's overarching purpose is to reveal God, including his plan and purposes for humans, but how do we make sense of that when we move down to some particular part of the overarching story, for example, Genesis 1? Are the details of this story,

16. "How Should We Interpret?"

some of which are propositions, insignificant for understanding God's plan and purposes for humans? Indeed Scripture is full of propositions about God, about humans, and about the relationship between God, humans, and creation as a whole. Whether one is looking at Genesis 1 or any other text it is difficult to see how the stories recorded can be easily severed from propositions embedded in those stories. Rather the propositions given in Scripture should be understood as integral to the larger purpose of revealing God and his relationship with and intentions for humans and creation as a whole. Consider the following examples:

> Hear O Israel, YHWH is God; YHWH is one. (Deut 6:4)

> In the beginning was the Word and the Word was with God and the Word was God. (John 1:1)

> If you confess with your mouth that Jesus is Lord and believe in your heart that God raised him from the dead, you will be saved. (Rom 10:9)

> God is light and in him is no darkness at all. (1 John 1:5)

Each of these texts represents a distinct genre embedded in the grand story of Scripture, the first in law, the second in a gospel, the third and fourth in epistles. Each text is also a proposition, telling something about God and either explicitly or by inference, our relationship with him.

Similar objections can be raised to the statement that Scripture is not a moral guidebook. Of course, Scripture's overarching intention is not to teach morality disconnected from the love of God for his people. Biblically, however, to love God is to obey him; to be called into relationship with the holy God entails living according to God's moral precepts, something that is at the heart of God's covenants. To be in right relationship with God is to live according to his revealed will. Relationship and obedience are two sides of the same coin. 2 Timothy 3:16–17 claims, "All Scripture is God-breathed and useful for teaching, rebuking, correcting and training in righteousness, so that the people of God may be thoroughly equipped for every good work." If we agree with Paul's instruction to Timothy, it seems that the whole of Scripture functions to teach God's people how to live in the presence of this holy God—although some texts are more specific in their moral instruction than others. For example:

> You shall love the LORD your God with all your heart, with all your soul, and with all your strength. (Deut 6:5)

He has shown you O man what is good. And what does the LORD require of you? To act justly and to love mercy and to walk humbly with your God. (Mic 6:8)

You have heard it said to the people long ago, "Do not murder, and anyone who murders will be subject to judgment." But I tell you that anyone who is angry with his brother will be subject to judgment. (Matt 5:21–22a)

So I say, live by the Spirit, and you will not gratify the desires of the sinful nature. . . .The acts of the sinful nature are obvious: sexual immorality, impurity, and debauchery; idolatry and witchcraft; hatred, discord, jealously, fits of rage, selfish ambition, dissensions, factions, and envy, drunkenness, orgies, and the like. (Gal 5:16, 19–21a)

Moral living or "training in righteousness," from a biblical perspective, is to live as God intended from the beginning, to live toward one's created *telos*. Jared Ortiz, in discussing Augustine's *Confessions*, makes the point that "for Augustine, there is no way to separate the ethical from the ontological."[17] Augustine is reflecting the wisdom of Scripture. To be what God intended humans to be is to live according to his design, a design codified in commandment as early as Genesis 3.

Along with these objections are those objections that Scripture is not a history or science book. While it is indeed the case that teaching science is not the overarching purpose of Scripture, it is not entirely true that Scripture doesn't tell us anything about the workings of the world around us and our relationship to the world. At the very least, we know from Scripture that all life comes from God, the source of life, and that he sustains his creatures right down to giving them food to eat (Exod 16; Pss 104:27–28; 145:15–16; 146:7; Matt 6:26, 30–44). As far as history goes, Scripture certainly does not record history in a modern fashion, but it does give us the history of salvation that includes the great salvific acts of God with his people. These major historic salvific acts are celebrated by devout Jews in the various feasts of the Old Testament and by Christians in the New Testament in the Lord's Supper. In this last feast, the greatest salvific act of all is re-presented to God's people regularly, bringing the work of God from the past into our present reality while looking forward toward the future restoration of all things.

17. Ortiz, "You Made Us for Yourself," 34.

Our approach to Scripture is very important. Most important is that we approach humbly, with a heart that is tuned to the Spirit's guidance, including how the Spirit has guided God's people throughout time and throughout the world. This approach demands that the text does not submit to us and our needs or ideas. We submit to the text. In other words, we don't come to the text demanding that it is not a certain sort of text or can't possibly be teaching us certain things. Rather, we come to the text with the assurance that the Spirit that testified through the words of the prophets and apostles recorded in Scripture is the same Spirit teaching us through those same words today.

The church has understood Scripture as God's self-revelation to humans. It is not uncommon to hear statements, however, that suggest that God also reveals himself in nature, so therefore we must take science seriously.[18] This idea is drawn from Romans 1, which affirms that some knowledge of God is indeed available through the creation. Paul writes in the context of a discussion of the wickedness of humans that "since the creation of the world God's invisible qualities—his eternal power and divine nature—have been clearly seen, being understood from what has been made, so that [humans] are without excuse" (Rom 1:20). As it interprets nature, science can indeed point to God's eternal power and divine nature, giving humans a cursory knowledge of God. Unfortunately, because of the corruption of the fall into sin, humans will, according to Paul, inevitably distort this knowledge, exchanging "the glory of the immortal God for images made to look like mortal man and birds and animals and reptiles" (Rom 1:23). Because of this warning against idolatry in Romans 1, the church has consistently recognized that while we can learn something about God from nature, the primary source of knowledge of God is Scripture. The reformer John Calvin calls Scripture the spectacles through which we must view God's self-revelation in creation. More specifically, in places where Scripture and creation collide, Scripture is used to correct creation with respect to knowledge of God, not the other way around.

That leads to another question, however. What about areas that are not directly concerned with knowledge of God's eternal power and divine nature? How, for example, do we handle collisions, tension, and disagreement between revealed knowledge about humans or the created world in

18. Young and Stearley, *Bible, Rocks, and Time*, 172. Davis and Stearley raise this issue at least in part because of the legitimate concern for the lack of respect or lack of curiosity among some Christians with respect to the findings of science.

general and knowledge received from science, philosophy, or other academic disciplines? Here is where many of the pastoral difficulties lie.

The majority of persons we encounter in church come to Scripture with a fairly literal hermeneutic. But a baldly "literal" hermeneutic may not, in some cases, be enough to grasp the meaning of some given text. More often than not, however, the literal is still a good starting point, even in English. What is most often the case as one comes to understand the historical context, grammatical nuances, and literary form of the text is not that the literal meaning is overturned or negated. Rather, one's sense of the text is deepened and broadened through more sophisticated interpretive practices. For example, one can read the story of Jesus calming the storm on the Sea of Galilee in the Gospel of Mark and be amazed at his power over the sea and his willingness to protect his disciples and their boat. But if we dig a bit deeper the meaning is broadened, and we find that Mark is not simply trying to show that Jesus is powerful and kind. A closer reading, one attentive to literary form and social context, discloses that it is only *after* Jesus calms the storm that the disciples are described as being "terrified." But such fear makes sense given that such first-century Jewish men would have known that only YHWH, Creator of heaven and earth, can control the waters in such a manner. This was not a miracle done by a mere man. Mark's deeper point, then, is that Jesus is Lord in a particular way that is illuminated by a first-century Jewish context. The meaning of the story has not changed, but rather it has *deepened* through the use of interpretive tools.

Two Stories

One rarely discussed approach to understanding the relationship between the story of science and that of Scripture is the idea that what we have are two stories that intersect at certain points but by and large stand in contrast with one another due to their discrepancies. Scientists may balk at the idea that evolution is a "story," but I do not mean to diminish the work of scientists or evolutionary theory in any way by such terminology. From the scientific side, I know that the evidence that scientists are working with is trustworthy, even though it is provisional by its very nature. The project of science is to find the best explanation possible given the physical evidence available. Change in thinking is inevitable either because the evidence changes in some way, perhaps with new evidence coming to light, or because previous theories that account for the evidence are disproved or expanded or modified or replaced to better account for what is observed. The evolutionary story that science offers is the best *physical* explanation of the history of life that we have, and it is grounded in an empirical understanding of knowledge. That does not mean, however, that there are no other ways to know or that experimental results that are testable and repeatable provide the only possible explanations or exhaustive explanations for what we know. Indeed, from the biblical side, I know that the Bible is trustworthy, and that it presents a very different picture of human life and origins, regardless of the general understanding that it is not a modern science textbook. This knowledge of the trustworthiness of the Bible is not based on an empirical framework but on the authority of the text due both to testimony of Scripture to its inspiration and to the inward testimony of the Holy Spirit. I see no need to try to reinterpret the story of Scripture in order to reconcile it with the story of science, any more than I see a need to reinterpret or deny the story of science in order to reconcile it with the story of Scripture. Both tasks are unhelpful for many people. Rather, one can affirm the story of Scripture alongside of the story of science, recognizing differences between the stories without shoehorning the details of one into the other and dishonoring both stories in the process. This is not an argument against attempts at harmonization. I am only arguing that harmonization is not necessary with respect to these two stories, depending on one's epistemic comfort with the difficulties that arise when comparing the two stories.

One example of two stories that have significant differences yet can be understood as compatible is the biblical story of creation as recorded in Genesis 1 and again in Genesis 2. Any observant reader will recognize the differences between these two stories. Indeed, these differences can evoke a level of discomfort within readers, as well as pressure to try to reconcile the two accounts. Biblical scholars have numerous theories about these differences, none of which are fully satisfying, but by now many agree that these are *complementary* accounts, as already noted in chapter 2. Each account presents the reality of creation from a different angle, including a different chronology of events. There are real differences between the two accounts. When read together, however, one gets a bigger picture of creation than when the two accounts are torn apart.

Why not use this example as a model to understand the two stories presented by Scripture and science? Because this book is about human persons, I will narrow the question down to the story of the development of human life on earth. When we look at this, it is clear that the differences between the story of science and the story of Scripture are profound. Scripture clearly presents the creation of humans as a deliberate and intimate act of God. Science clearly presents humans as gradually developing from a common animal ancestor. Scripture clearly presents the creation of two humans, a male and a female. Scientific evidence suggests that humans emerged as a group of somewhere between one hundred and a thousand persons. The list of particular differences could go on, but it is not hard to see that both accounts present the reality of human beginnings from vastly different perspectives. The differences between the stories cannot be easily resolved by suggesting that Scripture tells the story of "who" while science tells the story of "how." A close reading of Scripture, in fact, tells a "how" that includes God's self-deliberation and intimate molding of the first human from the dust of the ground, even breathing into the human "the breath of life." Maybe the tension felt when one reads the biblical account of creation alongside the scientific account of evolution has less to do with divergent pictures of human development than with a stubborn insistence by some that the two stories *must* somehow be reconciled. But what if each story offers a re-presentation of reality that, when placed side by side, appears paradoxical?

The *Oxford English Dictionary* defines a paradox as "an apparently absurd or self-contradictory statement or proposition, or a strongly counter-intuitive one, which investigation, analysis, or explanation may nevertheless prove to be well-founded or true."[19] While many philosophers and theologians are uncomfortable with paradox, the Christian tradition as a whole is not. This is especially true in the Eastern Orthodox tradition, which not only seems comfortable with the idea but embraces it. On the website of the Greek Orthodox Diocese of America, George Parsenios notes a connection between orthodoxy and paradox. "A paradox," he writes, "contradicts what we might commonly believe to be true. And Orthodox theology consistently presents us with things that contradict what we might commonly believe to be true. What is Orthodox," he asserts, "is often a Paradox."[20]

19. *Oxford English Dictionary*, s.v., "paradox." For my purposes here, I want to emphasize that the definition suggests a paradox is *"apparently"* self-contradictory. So, to say that both stories are true *appears* to be a self-contradictory statement but may, in fact, not be. We likely will not know the truth of the matter before we meet our Lord face to face, and perhaps we will never know.

20. Parsenios, "Orthodox Paradox."

He goes on to offer a number of examples that hold true whether one is a Western or Eastern Christian.

It is worthwhile to take a look at one of the examples Parsenios offers—the Christian understanding of the Trinity. We are monotheists, Christians insist. We worship but one God. And yet we worship three persons. God, in standard Christian orthodoxy, is both one and three. Standard orthodox theology asks believers to hold in tension both the "threeness" and the "oneness" of God, neither tipping too far in one direction or the other. Parsenios explains that "the Trinity is not just one person playing different roles, but three persons, Father, Son, and Holy Spirit, who are always three persons . . . and yet always One God." He summarizes: "In Orthodox theology, the rules of math do not apply. 3=1 and 1=3. What is Orthodox is Paradox."[21] Of course, this is not just true of Eastern Orthodox theology but of Christian theology in general, although Western theologians tend to push toward explaining the unexplainable while the East is much more content not only to embrace but also to adore the mysterious paradox. This is because mystery is reflective of the character of a God who is simultaneously hidden and revealed, transcendent and immanent.

The Christian tradition overall is rife with examples of paradox. Scripture tells us that Christ was born of a virgin, the dead will rise and live forever, power is perfected in weakness, and that glory comes in the form of a cross. Furthermore, Scripture gives examples of miracles that are seemingly contradicted by scientific data: a child is raised from the dead (2 Kgs 4:8–36); an axehead floats (2 Kgs 6:1–7); a dream is described by a person who did not himself have the dream (Dan 2:24–29); water is turned to wine (John 2:1–11); a storm is calmed with a word (Mark 4:35–41); a man walks on water (Matt 14:28–31). And, of course, these are just a few examples of biblical miracles that are deeply paradoxical when held up to the story of science. Quite often, when we enter the world of the text, we are challenged to set aside our rationalistic way of thinking and suspend our disbelief.

Paradox is also celebrated in some Christian songs. The contemporary song "Mary, Did You Know?" inspires wonder and challenges listeners to consider how it is that the human baby Mary holds could also be Almighty God.[22] In the late twentieth-century hymn, "Lord, You Are Both Lamb and Shepherd," hymnwriter Sylvia Dunstan affirms numerous dialectical paradoxes with respect to the incarnation of Jesus. For example, in the first verse

21. Parsenios, "Orthodox Paradox."
22. Lowry, "Mary, Did You Know?"

she describes Jesus as being both lamb and shepherd, prince and slave, peacemaker and swordbringer, as well as the everlasting instant.

Throughout her hymn she illustrates that paradox is central to our descriptions of Christ and in fact makes sense of Christ and his work in a way that defies logical explanation. James R. Payton writes, "The Orthodox emphasis falls not on speech about but on silence before God and his revelation." He goes on, "The person who would know God must drink deeply of, and not just analyze, what God has made known about himself and his ways toward humankind; one must be saturated with it through wonder rather than seek to connect its elements in curiosity."[23]

Perhaps the West has spent too much of its time in just such curiosity, seeking to connect the pieces and resolve the differences between the various elements of the story of science and the story of Scripture. In the process, we may have missed drinking deeply of the mystery not just of God, but of human persons, too. Insofar as humans are made in the image and likeness of the Mysterious One, it would make sense that humans are mysterious, too. Science simply can't give the full picture of humans any more than theology can offer a full picture of humans or of God. While a variety of harmonizations between the stories have been and will continue to be proposed and will be helpful to some, maybe another solution is to receive with thanksgiving the data of science that, for example, the first humans were a group ranging in number from one hundred to a thousand, while at the same time accepting by faith the biblical description of God creating a first couple, male and female in his image, who were subsequently tempted by an intruder and sinned against God.

One main difference between the knowledge we receive from Scripture and that which we receive from science is that much of the story of Scripture must be received by faith. Aquinas's insights are helpful given his use of reason or philosophical science, as he refers to it. Aquinas used the tools of natural reason available to him to help work out questions related to sacred doctrine. But when Scripture conflicted with reason, Scripture came out on top. Sacred doctrine is learned from divine revelation. Revealed truths, according to Aquinas, are not unreasonable but rather *exceed* reason. They reflect the nature of the incomprehensible God. Perhaps setting the stories of science and Scripture side by side is like looking at two works of art whose subject and artist are the same. One is a beautiful black and white photograph, the other a colorfully interesting abstract painting.

23. Payton, *Light from the Christian East*, 60.

In addition to the obvious differences between the two pieces, each work of art has a different name. It would be nearly impossible that a person could guess the subject was identical for both pieces apart from asking the artist. There may be places of overlap between the two works, but there are clearly great gaps between the stories these works of art tell as well. Nonetheless, each work of art re-presents the reality that is the subject.

Where science and Scripture are concerned, understanding each story as a re-presentation of reality offers the opportunity for affirming both stories on their own terms. Importantly, the two-story approach also allows the biblical text to once again stand on its own two feet without pressure from the story of science to overlay the biblical text with meanings that may ultimately be antithetical to its teaching. The two-story approach also recognizes and listens to the voice of the non-Western church that has read Scripture apart from the Enlightenment assumptions of the West. It also helps prevent complicating the meaning of the text to the point that the average reader of Scripture can no longer trust what they are reading without consulting the "experts."[24] To put it slightly differently, this two-story reading allows us to recognize that the story of Scripture comes with authority. It is, as the church for most of her history has affirmed, the very word of God and as such stands above all other authority. This does not mean that scientists cannot or should not do their work. It simply means that where the story of Scripture and the story of science are in tension with one another, we must, at the very least, allow people to live with the tension rather than insist that the tension be resolved.

Some suggest that mystery and paradox are cop-out categories for those who aren't willing to wrestle through to a full explanation. This has not, however, been the position of at least some parts of the historical church, as already noted. Mystery, as one author puts it, "bears witness to the immensity that awaits us."[25] Although here she is considering the mystery of our final state with God, it is important to remember that

24. I have in mind here, for example, current pressure on the text's presentation of a historic first couple and the suggestion that the doctrine of sin along with the biblical text must be reinterpreted to comport with scientific findings. One could also look at current presentations of human sexuality, an area where science is less definite yet those influenced by it are still willing to try to impose contemporary views of sexuality on the text (perhaps even suggesting that the biblical author did not know what we know today, a problem that flatly negates the position of those who believe that the primary author of Scripture is the Holy Spirit [2 Tim 3:15; 2 Pet 1:21]).

25. Siri, "Death and the Immensity."

whenever God is concerned, mystery is involved. The incomprehensibility and immensity of God entail mystery. Thus, mystery is a fitting category for the study of sacred science. Pastorally, this two-story approach I am proposing allows us to offer the laity as well as scholars, particularly those from the global church, the opportunity to fully appreciate both stories by recognizing them as mysteriously compatible.[26] This allows people the freedom to disagree gracefully while resting where they are epistemically comfortable, either in harmonization, apparent paradox, or somewhere in-between. Maybe embracing mystery and paradox where the stories of science and Scripture are concerned is not, to use Katherine Sonderegger's term, epistemic failure but, in fact, epistemic success.[27]

Conclusion

This chapter's focus has been primarily pastoral, focusing on the twin concerns of ensuring that (1) scientific findings concerning the development of life on earth, especially human life, are taken seriously, and (2) the biblical text is not forced into a science-inspired reinterpretation not fully faithful to the text. I identify this as a pastoral concern because, on the one hand, scientists have often been the subject of attack by Christians who feel threatened by findings that appear to contradict the biblical text. These Christians often overlook the fact that any number of scientists are our brothers and sisters in Christ who are following God's call and using their gifts to help us better understand the world around us. On the other hand, the findings of science have often led to general revelation superseding special revelation in an attempt to harmonize the two stories of science and Scripture. Indeed, in some cases the assumption is that whatever science discovers *must* entail reinterpretation, with exceptions sometimes (but not always) being made for miracles. This leaves many average Christians in a strange, pre-Reformation-like position of being unable to understand Scripture apart from some authority on the matter helping with the "true," albeit not obvious, meaning of the text.

This chapter has suggested that while harmonization of the two stories may be helpful for some, it is not uniformly helpful. Thus, for some

26. Sonderegger, *Systematic Theology* 1:89. Sonderegger is not using this phrase with reference to humans but with reference to the Trinity. I am merely borrowing her language and basic idea here but not her application.

27. I again borrow this language from Sonderegger, *Systematic Theology* 1:89.

Christians it may be more epistemically advantageous to recognize that science and Scripture portray two distinct stories of human development on earth. While these two stories may overlap at points, they quite often appear incompatible, but such incompatibility may be understood through the ideas of paradox or mystery. Rather than an intellectual cop-out, this should be seen as one way to help people recognize the validity of both stories, while maintaining the integrity of the plain meaning of the biblical text. Because paradox and mystery have a place in the Christian tradition, a retrieval of these concepts with respect to the stories of the development of life on earth should be embraced as one option to which people can turn for epistemic comfort.

5

Humans as Material-Spiritual, Intellective, Worshipping Animals

By NOW, WE HAVE looked at the question of human uniqueness from a variety of angles. We began with one traditional theological model, that of St. Thomas Aquinas. We then turned to Scripture, considering how humans are depicted in the biblical text. In the next chapter, we examined scientific data to help determine how humans are both similar to and very different from other animals from that perspective. While our explorations into science are by no means exhaustive, they do offer a reasonable picture of what might lead us to consider humans as unique from a scientific perspective. What is important to point out at this juncture is that regardless of whether we are looking at Aquinas, Scripture, or science, a reasonable case can be made that humans are not just unique in the sense that all kinds of animal are unique, but that humans are in fact *specially* unique, set apart and above the rest of creation. Indeed, the third chapter explored the idea that human capabilities and potentialities exceed those of other animals such that humans are distinct from other animals not just in degree, as some would argue, but in *kind*.

It is now time to bring the work I have done so far together. This chapter, therefore, will take the various insights from Aquinas, Scripture, and science and consider them as a whole, integrating the most important points gleaned from each section to suggest what exactly I mean when I argue that humans are specially unique. This chapter will therefore argue that humans—*all* humans—are specially unique because they are complex material-spiritual, intellective, worshipping beings, specially created by

God for the ultimate purpose of loving and worshipping God. In other words, humans are material-spiritual, intellective, worshipping animals. As noted in the introduction, any one of these characteristics by itself may not set humans apart from other animals. But the combination of all of these— a combination shared by *all* humans—marks *homo sapiens* as specially unique and distinct from other creatures in kind.

I will begin by discussing the claim that humans are *material-spiritual* beings, relying on the biblical argument from chapter 2. Then, using the foundation of Aquinas's understanding of the intellective soul, I will defend the claim that all humans, even the most profoundly intellectually disabled, are *intellective* beings, and I will explain not only how this is so, but why it is important. Finally, I will argue that humans are ultimately, and perhaps most importantly, *worshipping* beings, created for the ultimate end of communion with their Creator.

Humans as Material-Spiritual Beings

One thing that both the story of science and the story of Scripture agree on about humans is that humans are material beings. The assertion that humans are material needs little explanation because it is self-evident. Humans are made up of matter that can be seen, touched, tasted, and smelled. All humans, even the tiniest embryo, have mass and take up space. Affirmation that humans are material beings, however, is not identical to a materialist understanding of human persons. Materialist conceptions of human persons have become quite common, even in theological circles. Materialism suggests that humans are primarily or, in some cases, *only* material.

The move towards materialism stems primarily from challenges raised by modern neuroscience. The suggestion is that since neuroscientists have been able to explain in purely material terms many behaviors and characteristics once associated with a soul, the idea of a soul is no longer needed. Stephen G. Post writes, "Human capacities once attributed to a nonmaterial soul are now carefully mapped in various sections of the neurological substrate."[1] In other words, since we now know how brain processes work to bring about various human behaviors, suggesting that any particular behavior is in some way linked to or dependent on a soul is no longer necessary. For many scientists, but also for some philosophers, theologians, and biblical scholars, the idea of a soul has become obsolete.

1. Post, "Moral Case," 195.

Where scientists are concerned, it is true that they can examine things like how the brain operates in rational thought and religious impulses as well as any number of other neuropsychological phenomena. They can offer a multitude of interesting ideas about what might help humans and what might harm them based on their findings, and we are mostly better off because of these findings. But of necessity, they are only examining *material* processes—the brain and various neuronal connections—and how various behaviors relate to those material processes. Moving beyond those explanations, however, to suggest that human behaviors and attributes now can and must be explained by purely materialist neuroscientific models of one form or another is reductive, despite claims to the contrary.[2] Materialistic conceptions are reductionist, if for no other reason than that they methodologically disallow many nonmaterial realities of the kind a biblical worldview affirms.

The findings of science are based on a method that relies on observation of the physical, material world. Given that, science, due to its own boundaries, cannot make conclusions about the nonphysical world. In other words, scientists cannot give us information about or make judgments concerning the reality of immaterial souls, angels, demons, or "the spiritual forces of evil in the heavenly realms" (Eph 6:12). These creatures and phenomena are simply outside of the boundaries of science. Let me offer an example. It is not uncommon to hear the suggestion that demon possession as described in the New Testament was really a form of epilepsy or psychosis or some other type of mental illness. Those in the first-century, presumably including Jesus, just didn't know it as such but now, thanks to modern science, we do.[3] While in some cases Scripture does seem to describe a condition similar to what we now might diagnose as epilepsy or mental illness of some sort, not every case of demon possession in Scripture can be so easily placed into a medical or psychological category. Take, for example, the case of the Gerasene demonic found in both Mark 5:1–20 and Luke 8:26–39. In this story, Jesus directly addresses not the man, but the "epilepsy" or "psychosis" afflicting him, which apparently has a name:

2. See Madueme, "From Sin to the Soul." I agree with Madueme that Murphy's purported nonreductive physicalism ultimately fails in being truly nonreductive.

3. Indeed, I had a conversation on this topic with a professor of psychology at a well-known Christian university. It also seems that this rejection of a spiritual world—angels and demons—is a peculiarly Western phenomenon. Many people in other areas of the world, both Christian and non-Christian, fully affirm these spiritual beings, although they may refer to them with other terms.

Legion. Legion speaks back to Jesus, even requesting that "they" not be tortured but be thrown into some nearby pigs. Jesus, fully in control of the situation, grants that request, casting Legion out of the man and into a herd of pigs that subsequently runs headlong into the lake. In this case, if one suggests that the man's affliction is due to mental or physical illness, what precisely was it that Jesus spoke to and cast out of the man and into the pigs? If the man merely required healing of a disease, why all the theatrics? It appears that to relegate this man's torment to physical or mental illness is clearly to miss a good deal of what is going on in the story—Jesus's power over demons, one of the forces of evil in the world.

A problem similar to that of dismissing the reality of created, non-physical beings, such as angels and demons, arises when neuroscientists suggest that a soul does not exist or equate it with something emergent from the physical, akin to theory of mind discussed in chapter 3. Indeed, the shift in nomenclature from "soul" to "mind" may itself be indicative of the motivation to dismiss any traditional Christian notions of an immaterial soul. Just as science is unable to weigh in on the reality of demons in the story of the tormented Gerasene man, so also science cannot say anything about the presence or absence of an immaterial soul, although they may be able to discuss a mind, depending on how that term is defined. As with the presence or absence of immaterial beings, there is no way to test for the presence or absence of a soul and no way to draw conclusions about whether a soul might impact the neurological data under investigation. To claim that there is no evidence for the influence of an immaterial soul on some neural process bears a strong resemblance to suggesting there is no evidence for the influence of angels and demons in the world. While great strides have been made in understanding the workings of our brains, none of these strides necessarily eliminates the possibility that the neural operations of the brain are ultimately both configured by and operate in conjunction with an immaterial soul, similar to the holistic model described by Aquinas.

Regardless of the inability to test for or draw conclusions about the presence or absence of an immaterial soul, extensive arguments both for and against the reality of the soul have graced philosophical and theological literature for centuries. Some, as already noted, argue for a purely materialist conception of human persons. Others argue that brain processes like rationality, morality, and a relationship with God cannot be reduced to merely physical processes, yet they also reject traditional notions of a substantial, immaterial soul.[4] Still others, like myself, argue for some form of a subsistent soul. The range of possibilities is wide, and the discussion of this topic continues.[5] One observation of these ongoing discussions that is rarely addressed, however, is that on a very anecdotal level, it seems that most cultures throughout time and even today have had some sort of dualist conception of human persons.[6] Most people acknowledge a spiritual aspect to humans, as well as some form of ongoing spiritual existence. Psychologist Paul Bloom makes the point that it is "commonsense" for humans to believe in a soul, something he thinks is going to be difficult to rid ourselves of.[7] Similarly, philosopher Stewart Goetz argues that at least for the biblical authors, substance dualism is "commonsense," that is, it arises "out of the capacities of self-awareness (e.g., I am experiencing pleasure), sense perception (e.g., I see a tree), memory (e.g., I did not sleep well the past few nights), etc., which in part constitute human nature."[8] The fact that most people in most cultures do affirm a spiritual aspect of humans that continues to exist postmortem might suggest that this belief could be classified as "properly basic," along the same lines as belief in God, as proposed by philosopher Alvin Plantinga.[9]

Regardless of culture in general, however, the belief that humans are ensouled beings has been predominant through most of the history of the church. Some of the conceptions of human composition have been more

4. Murphy, "Nonreductive Physicalism," 116.

5. There are numerous works dealing with the topic of the soul. See, for example, Cooper, *Body, Soul, and the Life Everlasting*; Green and Palmer, *In Search of the Soul*; Corcoran, *Rethinking Human Nature*; Murphy, *Bodies and Souls, or Spirited Bodies*. More recently, Farris, *Introduction to Theological Anthropology*, 61–77.

6. In over thirteen years of teaching students from all over the world, I have asked my diverse group of students whether in their cultures, both within and outside of Christianity, people think there is some sort of spiritual entity in humans, the sort of thing that Christians have traditionally called a soul. I have yet to meet a student who has said no. This informal survey includes students from Mexico, China, Taiwan, Hong Kong, Korea, Nigeria, Kenya, Uganda, as well as many other countries. While it is merely anecdotal and has no scientific weight, it says something about the universality of this belief, whether described in Platonic or Cartesian terms, as is common in the West, or in other sorts of terms as is common outside of the West.

7. Bloom, *Descartes' Baby*, 209–27. See also Kärkkäinen, *Creation and Humanity*, 308. Bloom, to be clear, does think that we should rid ourselves of this primitive belief.

8. Stewart Goetz, "Substance Dualism," 125.

9. For a basic introduction to Reformed epistemology, including ideas like warranted belief and proper basicality, see Plantinga, *Knowledge and Christian Belief*, especially chap. 3. This would be worth further study.

compatible with the biblical text than others, but the overall affirmation of a human soul has been steady until relatively recently.[10] In addition, from the earliest days of the church, including the various writings of the New Testament, the church has affirmed a belief in some sort of continued disembodied existence after death while awaiting the final resurrection.[11] Jesus himself is presented in the New Testament as having existed somewhere between his crucifixion and resurrection (1 Pet 3:18–20). As Cooper writes, Jesus "died on Friday and was raised early on Sunday morning. During that interval either he was extinct until re-created on Easter or he existed in a nonfleshly intermediate state. Immediate resurrection is absolutely ruled out. For it was the body in the tomb that was raised."[12] In addition, to posit that Jesus went extinct after the crucifixion is to suggest that the two natures of Christ were somehow separated or that the second person of the Trinity went out of existence for a time. Either position is in direct contradiction to the early creeds of the church, as I have argued elsewhere.[13] Some sort of dualism that affirms ongoing disembodied existence postmortem is both historically and biblically defensible. The question, then, is not *whether* humans should be conceived of as having a body and soul, but which model of ensouled humans makes the best sense biblically and theologically.[14]

The answer to the question of what sort of body-soul unity humans are is debatable. From a biblical and theological perspective, however, I think that Aquinas's description best fits the perception of those who inhabited the world of the Bible as well as that of many people today. While Aquinas's understanding is often lumped together with all that is dualist and Greek, he actually offers a holistic conception of human persons quite similar to the "holistic-dualism" that Cooper proposes. As Cooper points out, Aquinas describes "an anthropology which was holistic, avoiding both the implication that a living person consists of two distinct entities and any antipathy between matter and form."[15]

---

10. See Cooper, *Body, Soul, and Life Everlasting*, 34–35.

11. For a detailed description of New Testament texts, see Cooper, *Body, Soul, and Life Everlasting*, especially chaps. 5–7. For some early church sources, see chap. 1 of the same volume. For a good overview of views of the afterlife among various groups in the first century, see chap. 12 of Wright, *New Testament in Its World*.

12. Cooper, *Body, Soul, and Life Everlasting*, 142.

13. Vanden Berg, "Impact of a Gap."

14. Goetz, "Substance Dualism," 127.

15. Cooper, *Body, Soul, and Life Everlasting*, 80.

As explained in chapter 1, Aquinas does affirm humans as consisting of matter and form, but, as Cooper points out, matter and form are one substance. Form—the spiritual aspect of humans—configures lifeless matter into a living human person. The form or "soul," for Aquinas, is what makes one alive, but this aliveness is intimately tied up with the body. Recall also that for Aquinas, the human soul is not generated by material and is not something inherited. The human soul is created by God to organize the matter for some particular person. In other words, my soul organizes the matter of my body. My soul is unique to me in a way similar to the way my genetic code is unique to me. Indeed, one could suggest, given Aquinas's framework, that God creates my soul to organize the material substance of the AGTC (the bases that make up DNA), which codes for various systems and structures of my body.

In addition, recall that for Aquinas, the soul is subsistent. In other words, the soul can exist apart from the body, albeit in a diminished way. This not only allows for the person's continued existence after death, as the church has always taught, but it also helps explain how the buried me and the resurrected me are one and the same person. Affirming a subsistent soul offers a depiction, albeit not a very detailed one, of what happens between death and the final resurrection. It can also help answer questions related to the resurrection. For example, what happens to those whose bodies are destroyed in some way, such as some of the victims of the Holocaust or those who choose cremation? Consider the body of a martyr, like Guido de Bres. After he was hanged for his Protestant beliefs, his body was burned, and the ashes were scattered on the Scheldt River. What will resurrection look like for De Bres? Or what about the bodies of those who were vaporized by the atomic bombs detonated at Hiroshima and Nagasaki, Japan? Aside from these rather dramatic illustrations of the problem resurrection might pose, it is also the case that for all of us, the longer our bodies remain in the grave the less there is of the original body. If a person's body is merely wrapped in cloth and laid in the dirt, eventually there will be little left that can be identified as a body. Of course, it is possible that God can gather up the molecules of one's body from wherever they might be and have one's soul reconfigure those same molecules into the person. But given the way that our bodies change over our lifetime, which person will that be? The cells that make us up when we die or some previous configuration of molecules? Will I be old and weak, middle aged, or get my twenty-year-old body back?

Changes in our bodies are part of life and indeed part of death. In his great resurrection text, the apostle Paul writes that there will be significant changes between the body that is "planted" and the one that is raised (1 Cor 15:35ff).

> The body that is sown is perishable, it is raised imperishable; it is sown in dishonor, it is raised in glory; it is sown in weakness, it is raised in power; it is sown a natural body, it is raised a spiritual body. (1 Cor 15:42–44)

But will these changes in one's body not also entail a change in the person's numerical identity?[16] There is no indication that they do when one affirms the existence of a substantial soul. Indeed, the physical changes in our bodies that happen throughout our lives, the decay that occurs after death, and even vaporization due to nuclear disaster are not a problem with the sort of holism suggested by Aquinas. Nor is "myself" at stake in the transformation between the current mortal body and the resurrected "spiritual" body. The continuity of the substance of the person lies not, first and foremost, with the body. The properties that constitute me or you or Mr. Rogers are guaranteed because the soul of the person that configures the matter (any matter) does not change, even with death. So whatever else might be meant by "spiritual body," what is certain is that this resurrected yet changed body is still me because it is configured by my soul.[17] Indeed throughout life, regardless of how one's body might suffer from injury or disease, the substantial soul does not change so the identity of the person does not change. Some capacities of the soul may never be actualized or may cease to be actualized, but the capacities remain because the soul remains. When woven together the biblical, historical, and theological affirmations of a soul are, at the very least, defensible against the continued criticism from various other disciplines.

16. Trenton Merricks helpfully describes numerical identity in terms of the qualities he had as a one-year-old and the qualities he has now. There is only one person in question—the one-year-old Merricks and the adult Merricks—despite different qualities or characteristics. Merricks, "Resurrection of the Body," 264.

17. The soul, then, is a substance. For more on what a substance is and how the properties of a substance relate to the substance through change, see Moreland and Rae, *Body and Soul*, 49–85.

Humans as Intellective

A holistic view of humans that includes a substantive soul is connected, for Aquinas, with the intellective capacity. Because my argument builds on Aquinas's ideas, it is worthwhile spending just a few lines reviewing Aquinas's understanding of capacities or potentialities of the soul as discussed earlier in chapter 1. The capacity that Aquinas thinks distinguishes humans from other material beings is the intellective capacity. As already noted, this is a capacity of the soul, not a physical capacity of a brain. Like a physical capacity, however, a capacity of the soul can be actualized or may lie dormant. For example, in the physical realm a person may have the physical capacity to become an Olympic-class swimmer. But what if that person does not live near any body of water large enough in which to learn to swim? Or what if she develops a fear of water at a young age and chooses not to learn to swim? In such cases, the physical capacity to swim, let alone at an Olympic level, will not be actualized. The capacities of the soul are something like that. While many of the capacities of the soul *require* the material of the body in order to be actualized, because the intellective capacity is immaterial and subsistent, it is not entirely dependent on the body for actualization. As noted in chapter 1, the human thinks by means of her intellect, the brain or body simply supports this activity. After death the soul leaves the body, but the intellective capacity is still able to function in this disembodied state because it is supported by God. For Aquinas, affirming the soul as intellective is important because the intellective capacity is at the core of what makes humans like God, that is, their ability to think, reflect, and understand. Thus, Aquinas also associates the soul with the image of God, which includes human likeness to God.

Aquinas's description of the image of God falls into the category of structural understandings of the image of God. The structural view of the image places the focus on, as Joshua Farris writes, "specific features or properties or capacities (e.g., consciousness, freedom of the will, and the soul)."[18] In recent years, structural views like that of Aquinas have fallen out of favor. There are any number of reasons for this, ranging from the charge that it is not biblically supported, to the supposed dependence of the early church fathers on Greek philosophical thinking that held rationality up as

---

18. Farris, *Introduction to Theological Anthropology*, 85. Farris offers a wonderfully brief summary of the three main views of the image of God on pp. 84–89.

the highest good.[19] More recently, structural views that identify intellect as the key capacity that characterizes humans as human have been criticized by those who suggest that the focus on intellect marginalizes those who are cognitively disabled.[20] Nonetheless, it is worth reconsidering whether disposing of all structural views of the image is warranted, especially since these views have been dominant throughout the history of the church. In order to do this, I will begin by offering a brief review of the two other main views of the image of God.

As noted in chapter 2, the most prevalent view among Old Testament scholars is the functional view. Richard Middleton, for example, suggests a "royal-functional" reading of Genesis 1:26–27. By this he means that humans are both delegated by God to rule and that in their rule they represent God and thus possess a functional similarity to God.[21] This view, it is argued, most closely approximates the language and thought of the Genesis text itself. The other prevalent view is the relational view. This view suggests that, rather than focusing on capacities or God's tasking of humans to rule the earth, the focus should be on humans in relationship to God and others. As Farris writes, this model focuses on "the situatedness of the human in relation to God and his design for his creatures."[22] Some form of the relational view has been at the forefront of theological discussions at least since Barth, who offered one version of this view, and it has been widely accepted by theologians, at least since the publication of Stanley Grenz's seminal work on the topic.[23]

One problem that arises with both the functional and relational views is that they appear to preference what a human *does* over what a human *is*. To be, in each case, is to function in a certain way or to be in relation to something. There is no capacity inherent to the person that identifies the person as human. As Farris writes, "It is not clear that the views [functional and relational] are sufficient in themselves."[24] What, for example, allows one to function as a royal representative? And what if a person is unable to

19. For a complete critique along these lines, see Grenz, *Social God and Relational Self*, 142–62.

20. See, for example, Cortez, *Theological Anthropology*, 20; John Swinton, *Dementia*, 11.

21. Middleton, *Liberating Image*, 88.

22. Farris, *Introduction to Theological Anthropology*, 88.

23. Grenz, *Social God and Relational Self*.

24. Farris, *Introduction to Theological Anthropology*, 89.

function in that way? In other words, function requires structure, at least at some level. And what exactly defines a human as human just because they are in relation to something or someone else? Isn't every created thing situated in relation to every other created thing? What is it that makes this created thing—humans—what they are? What about them makes them human?

Anthony Hoekema also recognized this problem and suggested that *both* structure *and* function are necessary for understanding the image of God.[25] He clarifies that "we may say that by the image of God in the broader or structural sense we mean the entire endowment of gifts and capacities that enable man to function as he should in his various relationships and callings."[26] Hoekema is not narrowing the image to just one particular capacity. Rather, his definition of the structural image points to *all* of our capacities in a way similar to that of Aquinas. While I agree with Hoekema that all of our capacities are part of the structural image of God in humans, I also side with Aquinas's view that it is the *intellective* capacity that sets us apart in some ways from other creatures. Indeed, although Aquinas likely did not think in these terms, the scientific data pointed out in chapter 3 suggests that the human ability for reasoning, self-transcendence, morality, language, and culture creation is not only unique to humans but is connected to our intellective capacity.[27] In addition, the intellective capacity is central to our ability to function both as royal rulers and in various relationships. Oliver O'Donovan writes, "Knowledge is the root of [human] authority over his fellow creatures, as it is also the root of the communion which each human being enjoys with his fellow humans."[28] In summary, to function as God's representative rulers is itself an aspect of the human relationship to the rest of creation and is dependent in certain ways on the intellective capacity. Because of that, it will be helpful to delve a bit more into human relationality and the intellective capacity.

25. Hoekema, *Created in God's Image*, 69.

26. Hoekema, *Created in God's Image*, 70–71.

27. Of course, for scientists the intellective capacity is limited to the brain, whereas Aquinas associates this capacity with the soul, assisted by the brain, as already noted.

28. O'Donovan, *Resurrection and Moral Order*, 81.

Intellective Capacity and Human Relationality

Various things are meant by the phrase "human relationality." Sometimes, as Farris suggests, relationality points to the situatedness of humans in creation. That is fine so far as it goes. But biblically, relationality is not a general statement of humans as situated within creation. Biblical depictions of human relationality most often have to do with stories that disclose something about human interpersonal relationships, including and most importantly their relationship with God. Indeed, Grenz's portrayal of the relational nature of humans was directly tied to the communion of the persons of the Trinity.[29]

When we move from relationality as human situatedness to relationality as portrayed in Scripture or theology, we can begin to recognize the essential connection between knowing and relationships. It would be difficult to conceive of, for example, intertrinitarian communion apart from intertrinitarian knowing. In a similar way, knowing is central to healthy interpersonal relationships. We form relationships with others in a large part in order to know and be known. Even Facebook friends generally "know" or hope to know something about each other at some level, despite lists of hundreds of "friends." In general, relationships grow deeper as persons come to know each other better. In good marriages, for example, it is not unusual for spouses to finish each other's sentences, order food or drinks for one another when they step away, or buy personal gifts for one another because they know each other so well. Conversely, knowing some people whose particular traits may be detrimental to us helps us avoid those people and thereby avoid further harm. Both who we choose to be in a relationship with and who we reject are often based on knowing. Relationality and knowing go hand in hand.

Like human relationships, then, knowing God is at the heart of a loving relationship with God. Human knowledge of God comes in and through a relationship with God, a relationship initiated by God and to which humans respond. Herman Bavinck makes clear that knowledge is not mere proposition but tied to relationship. He writes that faith "is in essence and from the start a personal relationship with God."[30] This is evident in Scripture. God makes himself known to Abraham (Gen 12), eventually confirming this relationship with a covenant that will include Abraham's

---

29. Grenz, *Social God and Relational Self*, 53–57.
30. Bavinck, *Reformed Dogmatics*, 4:112.

children (Gen 15; 17). Later, God remembers his covenant with Abraham when he hears the suffering of his people in Egypt. He reveals himself to Moses as the God of Abraham, Isaac, and Jacob, promising to bring these descendants of Abraham into the land he had promised (Exod 3). Why will God do this for these people? To fulfill his promise to Abraham, but also because "Then you will know that I am the LORD your God" (Exod 6:7). Indeed, throughout the Old Testament God's mighty works, works of both salvation and judgment, are associated with people coming to know that he is YHWH (e.g., Exod 14:4; Josh 4:24; 1 Sam 17:47; Ezra 6:7, 10, 13, 14). The world will *know* God because they have witnessed and experienced his work.

The importance of knowledge of God in a relationship with him is highlighted in the prophet Isaiah. John Oswalt writes that "*know* is a covenant word."[31] In other words, it is a *relational* word. Israel knows God because they have experienced God. Isaiah opens with a comparison between Israel and domesticated animals. "The ox knows his master, the donkey his owner's manger, but Israel does not know, my people do not understand" (Isa 1:3). The lack of knowledge of God by his own people is not only presented as ludicrous in this comparison, but as reason for judgment. Whereas dumb animals know to whom they belong and who cares for them, Israel does not.[32] Throughout the book of Isaiah, as well as many of the other eighth-century prophets, Israel's ability to know God is contrasted with her willful not knowing. Lack of knowledge is a hindrance to right relationship with God and is something one is culpable for. To know God is to love God, and to love God is to obey him.

This same line of thought follows into the New Testament. Love is connected to knowledge and obedience and the "Spirit of truth" (John 14:9, 15–17). The world does not know the Spirit but the disciples "know him, for he lives with you and will be in you" (John 14:17). A bit later in the Gospel of John, Jesus prays, "this is eternal life: that they may know you, the only true God, and Jesus Christ, whom you have sent" (John 17:3). In addition, similar to the mission expressed in the Old Testament, Paul speaks about Christians spreading everywhere "the knowledge of Christ" (2 Cor 2:14) and expresses his own desire to "know Christ and the power of his resurrection" (Phil 3:10). Earlier in Philippians, he connects love and knowledge, praying that the people's love "may abound more and more in

31. Oswalt, *Book of Isaiah*, 86.

32. Oswalt, *Book of Isaiah*, 86.

knowledge and depth of insight" (Phil 1:9). As with the Old Testament, love and knowledge are deeply connected. Overall, Scripture portrays knowledge as integral to relationships, most especially one's relationship with God. Thus, to refer to the image of God solely in terms of relationship seems to overlook the overarching biblical connection between knowledge and relationships, including one's relationship with God. In addition, the assertion that the emphasis of the tradition on knowing is a harbinger of the influence of Greek philosophy overlooks the clear biblical evidence for the importance of knowing for our relationship with God. Since relationality is a legitimate way to understand how humans image God and relationships are built from knowledge, it doesn't seem a far stretch to suggest that knowledge is not only one way humans image God, but also that the intellective capacity is what grounds our ability to have a relationship with God and others.

Intellective Capacity and Disability

One of the other main concerns of many arguments against intellective understandings of the image of God is that focusing too much on the ability to know and reason has the potential to marginalize persons with cognitive disabilities or mental illness. These concerns must be taken seriously. But does replacing the focus on the intellect with a focus on function or relationship actually alleviate the problem of marginalization or dehumanization of those with diminished cognitive abilities? Even a brief survey of man's inhumanity to man would suggest otherwise, whether one is looking at Christians or non-Christians. For example, is it really plausible to think that had the prevalent model of the image of God been relational rather than intellective that Christian slaveowners in the south would have seen their African slaves as human? I don't think so. Whether based on race, or class, or tribe, or sexual behaviors, history amply demonstrates that humans have bottomless resources for lifting up their own sort of persons, while at the same time dehumanizing those who do not measure up to their category of humanness. Pigeonholing the image of God into a single category, whether that category is some form of intellective, functional, or relational, is unhelpful for preventing the dehumanization of the "other." Noreen Herzfeld offers a way forward in thinking about this. She suggests, in a way similar to suggestions dealing with atonement theories, that rather than asserting an either/or way to understand humans in the image of God, a both/and approach would be better.

Herzfeld notes that the three main interpretative traditions of the image of God—the substantive [structural], the functionalist, and the relational—each have different sources of authority and different methodologies.[33] Each, therefore, offers a different approach to understanding humans and the image of God fully. She also suggests that the three approaches are "not necessarily mutually exclusive."[34] Each view correctly recognizes some important aspect of how humans are like God, but each on its own is incomplete. Tearing intellect, function, and relationality apart fails if for no other reason than that these characteristic elements of human existence are ineluctably interrelated, whether one is discussing the image of God or humans more generally.

To say that relationality, function, and intellect are intertwined is simply to acknowledge that most of what we do as humans cannot be easily isolated into only one area of the person, or even one area of the brain given what we know about how humans actually process operations. Therefore, I suggest that a retrieval of the intellective approach offered by Aquinas allows for a holistic understanding of the image of God where each of the various approaches—intellective, functional, relational—are necessary but none by itself sufficient for depicting the complexity of the image of God. Indeed, each of these three approaches offers a glimpse of how humans are like God.[35] And while none of these models can stand on its own, like Aquinas, I suggest that the intellective model is foundational, in part because the intellective capacity is deeply tied to our ability to function in relationship with God.

Retrieval and Beyond

According to Aquinas, the image of God is associated with the soul. Recall that for Aquinas the type of soul that animates humans—an intellective

---

33. Herzfeld, *In Our Image*, 31.

34. Herzfeld, *In Our Image*, 32.

35. Likeness to God is an important facet of Barth's relational view as well the functional and intellective views. While many modern exegetical treatments downplay any difference between image and likeness, older treatments, some of which recognize the parallel structure, still suggest that these terms are both closely related and somewhat distinct in how they should be understood. Aquinas is one such exegete.

soul—is what distinguishes them from other living things. The intellective capacity of the soul is unique to humans. It is the intellective capacity that gives humans the ability not just to know in general, but to know and love God, the highest good. Two characteristics of the intellective capacity are important. The first characteristic is the fact that the soul, including its intellective capacities, survives death. Because of this, the person postmortem is able to continue to know and love God. Indeed, Scripture indicates that this postmortem knowing of God will surpass our ability to know God in this life (1 Cor 13:12). This is a comfort to those who face death, whether their own or that of a loved one who dies in Christ. Second, and moving beyond Aquinas's own view, the knowledge that one's soul survives death might also offer comfort in this life for persons with cognitive disabilities or mental illness and those who love them.

As noted above, a focus on intellective capacities and knowing has been criticized in recent years as sidelining or ignoring people with cognitive disabilities. For example, Hans Reinders presents to his readers the story of a severely cognitively disabled young woman named Kelly. Because Kelly has microcephaly, a condition with a severely damaged brain, she was unable to do much of anything other than breathe. Furthermore, "Kelly never had, and never will have, a sense of herself as a human being."[36] So far as anyone can tell, Kelly does not even know that she exists. Simply put, Kelly has fewer outward characteristics of being human than the bonobos we considered in chapter 3. Regardless of outward characteristics, however, from the perspective of Aquinas, Kelly is a material-spiritual being animated by an intellective soul with all the capacities that entails. Unfortunately, very few of these capacities can be physically actualized because of her disability.

However, one capacity does not actually require the body in order to be actualized, at least according to Aquinas. Recall that for Aquinas, although the intellective capacity needs the support of the body to think, when separated from the body at death it can still operate, albeit with the support of God. If this is the case after the soul is separated from the body by death, could it not also be possible that in certain cases the intellect can operate apart from the body even in life, despite physical limitations? In other words, contrary to those who suggest that insistence on an intellective soul diminishes or even dehumanizes those who are cognitively impaired,

36. Reinders, *Receiving the Gift*, 21.

affirmation of a human soul with intellective capacity that can operate apart from the body may offer a more positive portrayal.

Some theologians like Reinders suggest that while Kelly cannot know God, God still knows and loves Kelly. Fair enough. But what if there is more? Consider Aquinas's understanding of separated souls. Aquinas is clear that the proper existence for a human soul is to be united to the body and a soul that is separated from the body exists in a diminished state.[37] That does not mean, however, that a separated soul cannot acquire knowledge. Rather, as Davies explains, "He [Aquinas] is convinced that even a 'separated soul' is a human soul, but he is equally convinced that it cannot acquire knowledge as a human being in the world does."[38] "It is possible," writes Aquinas, "for it [the soul] to exist apart from the body, and also to understand in another way."[39] In his reply to the objection that separated souls apart from the body know nothing, Aquinas acknowledges the problem but argues that "the soul in that state understands by means of participated species arising from the influence of divine light, shared by the soul as by other separate substances, though in a lesser degree."[40] In other words, again according to Davies, Aquinas thinks that after death and before the resurrection, our souls "can have knowledge by virtue of God's direct action."[41] Davies goes on to explain that what Aquinas means is that

> God directly causes separated souls to have knowledge, that God, just by fiat, brings it about that they understand in some way. Aquinas is clear that this action of God results in knowledge that arises in a way that differs from that by which living human beings acquire knowledge, yet he evidently takes it to be possible knowledge. He sees it as God's knowledge shared with human souls by the creative activity of God.[42]

Aquinas does not go into detail about how this can be the case and, according to Davies, does not purport to do so. Rather, he bases his ideas on his understanding of revelation "that something of us survives even before

---

37. Aquinas, *ST*, Ia 89.
38. Davies, *Thomas Aquinas's Summa*, 146.
39. Aquinas, *ST*, Ia 89 co.
40. Aquinas, *ST*, Ia 89 ad 3.
41. Davies, *Thomas Aquinas's Summa*, 146.
42. Davies, *Thomas Aquinas's Summa*, 146.

we are raised" and that "something"—our soul—can enjoy God between death and the final resurrection.[43]

Even Aquinas does not think this is provable and, according to Davies, thinks that understanding souls such as these are beyond philosophy. But suppose Aquinas is right about separated souls? If separated souls can know and love[44] God in the time between death and the resurrection, why could not something similar be the case for those who have limited sensory abilities in this life? Could not God act directly to make himself known to them in order that they could know and love him? Might Kelly not just be *known by* God, but *know* and *love* God too through the power of the Spirit working with her intellective soul?

In other words, just as the disembodied intellective soul postmortem is able to know and love God with God's assistance despite its diminished state, so the intellective soul in a cognitively disabled person would operate with God's assistance in a diminished state because of the person's profound physical limitations. Whatever else that diminished state might include, however, it would certainly include one's ability to be in a relationship with God, that is, to know and love God despite the physical and sensory limitations. Indeed, through the power of the Spirit, God, by divine fiat, could make himself known to persons with these limitations. More specifically, regardless of whether one is speaking about persons whose brains are not fully formed, as is the case with an embryo, or about someone like Kelly whose brain is malformed, or about those whose brains no longer show signs of knowing (like those with various forms of dementia), or persons with severe brain injuries, or those in a persistent vegetative state, or someone with a severe mental illness that hinders their ability to comprehend reality, there is no reason to believe that these persons are nonetheless able not just to *be* known, but to know and love God in return.[45] They are able to participate in an interpersonal relationship with their Creator, a key component of God's intention for humans. Matthew Levering suggests

---

43. Davies, *Thomas Aquinas's Summa*, 146.

44. Although Davies uses the idea of enjoying God in the intermediate state, it seems to me that enjoyment entails knowledge and love of God. So I will speak of knowing and loving God, assuming that in our knowing and loving, in this life or the next, we also enjoy or take delight in God.

45. This is a key difference between theologians like Reinders and Swinton, on the one hand, and myself, on the other. While I think it is wonderful to be known by God and that, in fact, happens prior to any knowing on my part, the *telos* of humans is not merely *to be known and loved* by their Creator, but *to know and love* God in return.

that Aquinas and at least some of the church fathers would affirm this. He writes, "For Aquinas (and the fathers), even if the powers of the soul are not in act [actualized] or are unable in this life ever to be in act due to a bodily defect, the grace of the Holy Spirit can still transform the soul and elevate the person relationally to union with the persons of the Trinity."[46]

For some, all of this will look like nothing more than wishful thinking. But *if* one accepts Aquinas's holistic notion of human persons as material-spiritual beings animated and configured by an intellective soul, and *if* that person's soul is separated from the body at death but continues to be able to know and love God, then it does not seem too far a stretch to consider that persons whose brains are malformed and/or unable to operate normally might also have their intellect supported by God for the purpose of relationship with him. Indeed, this is the very thing humans were created for: to know and love God. So why wouldn't God provide a way for all humans to do this?

On a personal level, my father suffered with dementia for fifteen years. He accepted what was happening to him with faith in God and a grace-filled spirit. Toward the end of his earthly journey, he no longer knew most of his family members, including me. Sometimes he did not even know his wife of more than sixty years. He could no longer speak; he could no longer sing. But I never doubted for a minute that while he sat with his eyes closed, he was communing with God. It is what he had done his whole life, and there was no reason to think that as he peacefully sat in his chair, that was exactly what he was doing. I was sure of it. Was this wishful thinking on my part? I don't think so. There was evidence on occasion that this is indeed what he was doing. In addition, I cannot even imagine that his damaged brain was able to hinder his lifelong interpersonal relationship with his Lord—a relationship, indeed *the* relationship, for which he was created.

Humans as Worshipping Beings

Many theological traditions have pointed out that humans are created in a threefold relationship: with God, with other humans, and with creation. The primary relationship, as I have already discussed, is one's relationship with God. This is the human's primary relationship because, as Hoekema writes, a human is a creature "who owes [her] existence to God,

46. Levering, *Engaging the Doctrine of Creation*, 174.

is completely dependent on God, and is primarily responsible to God."[47] In this relationship, God makes himself known to humans, and humans are intimately known by God (Ps 139). It is out of this relationship that the human's ultimate purpose flows. Hoekema explains, "To be a human in the truest sense . . . means to love God above all, to trust him and obey him, to pray to him and to thank him."[48] In some sense, human relationships with others and with creation are dependent on our relationship with the living God. "We love because he first loved us" (1 John 4:19).

To be human is to be the image of God. As the image of God, proper human function is to represent God and reflect God's glory to the world. Bavinck writes, "We are only truly human to the extent that we display God."[49] And G. K. Beale adds that "Adam and Eve and their progeny were created to be in God's image in order to reflect his character and glory and fill the earth with it."[50] Humans are the image of God, and as such they are intended by nature to function as the image of God—reflecting God's own attributes and mediating his presence in their call to rule as vice-regents. In the Reformed tradition, the Westminster Larger Catechism teaches this notion of human *telos* in its first question and answer. "What is the chief and highest end of man? Man's chief and highest end is to glorify God and enjoy him forever."[51] The ultimate purpose of human existence is a relationship with God characterized by glorifying him.

Glorifying God is very similar to worshipping him. In Psalm 29, the psalmist exhorts those listening:

> Ascribe to the LORD, O mighty ones,
> ascribe to the LORD glory and strength.
> Ascribe to the LORD the glory due his name;
> worship the LORD in the splendor of his holiness. (Ps 29:1–2)

The psalmist is not asking that the heavenly beings and God's gathered people attribute something to YHWH that is not rightly his. Completely the opposite. The psalmist is commanding those gathered to attribute to YHWH what is due him, to give him what he deserves: glory. And what is glory? The Hebrew word literally means "to be heavy, weighty, burdensome,

---

47. Hoekema, *Created in God's Image*, 75.
48. Hoekema, *Created in God's Image*, 76.
49. Bavinck, *Reformed Ethics*, 4:40.
50. Beale, *We Become What We Worship*, 128.
51. *Westminster Larger Catechism* 1.

honored."[52] The Greek word *doxa* carries similar connotations including fame, renown, honor, and splendor, and it is associated with the action of praising or magnifying someone.[53] The call to give God glory and praise crescendos in the early verses of this psalm in something of a call and (implied) response fashion:

Psalmist	Give to the LORD you "mighty ones"[54]
Congregation	Give him what?
Psalmist	Give the LORD glory and strength
Congregation	Why?
Psalmist	Glory is due his name, that's why
Congregation	What does that look like?
Psalmist:	Worship!!

Giving glory to God comes with the call to worship him and only him. Ascribing glory to God is one aspect of worshipping of him.

Worship is an inherently religious activity. By that I mean that worship draws us beyond ourselves and our immediate story to something that transcends us and gives life meaning. Christian Smith makes the case that humans are believing animals. By this he means, at least in part, that we are creatures who inhabit stories. Indeed, we "tell and retell narratives that themselves come fundamentally to constitute and direct our lives."[55] Christian corporate worship is a rehearsal of one particular story—the story of humans in relationship with God. It is a weekly reminder of the human story, a story of creation, fall, redemption, and consummation. To put it another way, the Christian story is the story of human beings created for relationship with God, turning away from God and rejecting that relationship, and God becoming one of us to restore the possibility of relationship with him, the possibility of new creation. John Witvliet writes, "Christian liturgy is fundamentally an act of *anamnesis*, an act of rehearsing God's actions in history: past and future, realized and promised."[56] In addition, corporate worship prepares us for a life of worship, a life shaped by the fact that we are images of God called to reflect and represent God to the

52. Brown, Driver, and Briggs, *Hebrew and English Lexicon*, s.v. "kābôd."
53. Gingrich and Danker, *Greek-English Lexicon*, s.v. "doxa, doxadzo."
54. Literally "sons of God."
55. Smith, *Moral, Believing Animals*, 64.
56. Witvliet, "Trinitarian DNA," 7.

world around us in all that we do. To put it a bit differently, both corporate practices and the intentional habits of a life of worship are formational.

In addressing the topic of formation, I have in mind specifically Christian formation. Christian formation is the process of becoming what God intended humans to be from the beginning. Although humans never ceased to be the image of God, we did cease to function properly as the image of God after the fall into sin. Even after human rebellion against him, however, God pursued humans in love, wooing us in his direction to the life he intended. In the broad Christian tradition, life is often understood in terms of movement either toward or away from God. Scripture, especially wisdom literature, refers to this movement in terms of a path or way. One is either on the path of life or the path of death. The path of life is grounded in the law, part of God's covenant stipulations to maintain the relationship between humans and God. The path of death is grounded in disobedience associated with disregard for our covenant relationship with God (Ps 1). In the New Testament, it becomes even more clear that human destiny is aligned with conformity to Christ (Rom 8:29), the preeminent image of God. It is also clear that who or what one worships makes all the difference in whether one is on the path of life, associated with conformity to the image of God, or the path of death—that is, whether she is becoming more like the image of God or less like that divine image.

The idea that worship forms humans in one way or another is clear in Scripture, perhaps nowhere more so than in Psalm 115:2–8. These verses are a poetic warning that is repeated almost verbatim in Psalm 135:15–18. The psalmist begins Psalm 115 by reminding listeners that only YHWH is deserving of glory. "Not to us, O Lord, not to us but to your name be the glory," sings the psalmist. Cornelius Plantinga writes that when it comes to glory, "we think glory is all about making a splash."[57] We are drawn to people and things who attract our attention, that appear magnificent. "In ordinary life glory is reputation. It is reputation built on competition and publicity and peer review by people just as screwed up as we are."[58] A good deal of the problem with giving and receiving glory is that glory and worship are so tightly related that giving glory to someone other than God nearly always entails worship. Yet this is what humans often do. Humans seem inclined to worship something, but as Plantinga notes, what we are inclined to worship is often something or someone that makes a splash,

57. Plantinga, "Deep Wisdom," 150.
58. Plantinga, "Deep Wisdom," 151.

that lights up our horizon, that appears superlative in one way or another. The psalmist seems well aware of this as he goes on to contrast worship of YHWH with idolatry. What is striking in this psalm is the psalmist's warning that what humans worship will impact their lives.

> Why do the nations say, "Where is their God?"
>> Our God is in heaven; he does whatever pleases him.
> But their idols are silver and gold,
>> made by the hands of [humans].
> They have mouths but cannot speak,
>> eyes but they cannot see;
> they have ears, but cannot hear,
>> noses, but they cannot smell;
> they have hands, but cannot feel,
>> feet, but they cannot walk;
>> nor can they utter a sound with their throats.
> Those who make them will be like them,
>> and so will all who trust in them. (Ps 115:2–8)[59]

The message of this psalm is dark. Worship is the proper action of humans. It springs from who we are created to be. But when we worship the wrong object, exchanging the glory of God for something else instead of conforming toward the image and likeness of God as he intends, we become like the lifeless, inhuman idols we have chosen instead (Rom 1). In the words of G. K. Beale, "We become what we worship."[60]

Beale points out that this basic concept is not isolated to a few texts. The notion that we become what we worship runs throughout Scripture. Humans are worshipping beings created for a relationship with God characterized by worshipping and glorifying him. When we do this, we move toward the life that God intended humans to have, a life characterized by our created nature as images of God. Beale writes that "God has made humans to reflect him, but if they do not commit themselves to him, they will not reflect him but something else."[61] The principle, asserts Beale, is that "we resemble what we revere, either for ruin or restoration."[62]

The ultimate purpose of humans is to glorify God in all of life. The first humans rebelled against that purpose when they chose to glorify

59. These same words, nearly verbatim, are also part of Ps 135.
60. Beale, *We Become What We Worship*, 21, 22, 46.
61. Beale, *We Become What We Worship*, 16.
62. Beale, *We Become What We Worship*, 49.

themselves by eating from the forbidden tree so they could become like God. They were not satisfied with reflecting God's glory. They wanted their own. They did this to their ruin, as well as to the ruin of their progeny and creation itself. But God in his infinite mercy did not leave humans alienated from him. In Abram, God chose a people for himself who would reflect his glory to the world, drawing all people to him. Through his covenant, God guarantees that despite the infidelity of his people, he will maintain faithfulness in his relationship with them. He chose to become one of us to restore us and all creation for his glory. When humans turn back to God in Christ through the power of the Spirit, we can once again reflect God's glory to the world.

The apostle Paul writes that Christians are being transformed by the Spirit throughout our lives into the image of our Lord Jesus Christ (2 Cor 3:18). Like Moses after he had been with God on the mountain, we reflect God's glory and so our transformation comes with "ever increasing glory." What Psalm 115 warns us of however, is that when we choose to worship something other than YHWH, we reflect that other god to the world because we take on the characteristics of that god. Beale writes, "If people are committed to God, they will become like him; if they are committed to something other than God, they will become like that thing, always spiritually inanimate and empty like the lifeless and vain aspect of creation to which they have committed themselves."[63] Instead of life and restoration, we will reflect death. Instead of displaying the glory of God to the world, we will display the false glory of idols. Humans are worshipping beings, created for the purpose of glorifying God.

Does this idea of humans as worshipping beings end up disqualifying some from being human, perhaps the same folks who were mentioned in our discussion of humans as having intellective capacity? Can, for example, Kelly or my severely demented father worship God? If we allow that their souls have an intellective capacity, a capacity that allows them to know and love God despite physical limitations, I think that the answer is yes. In fact, given that they do not have to deal with the distractions of life that constantly draw us away from communion with God, it seems reasonable to suggest that both Kelly and my father may know and love God, and they may therefore glorify God in ways that are more focused and full than we can even imagine. Persons like Kelly and my father, in other words, are also worshipping beings.

63. Beale, *We Become What We Worship*, 284.

Conclusion

This chapter has sought to paint a picture of humans—all humans—as material-spiritual, intellective, worshipping beings, and therefore as specially unique creations within the world. Drawing on our biblical work in chapter 2 as well as what we learned from Aquinas, we began by describing humans as holistic body-soul creatures. I argued that despite modern academic distaste for affirming the existence of a soul, the idea of humans as material-spiritual beings is supported by the biblical text both in the Old and New Testaments. In addition, this has been the belief of the historic Christian church throughout its existence as well as being generally accepted across many cultures.

We also affirmed Aquinas's assertion that humans are intellective creatures. By this he means that humans, unlike other beings, have an intellective capacity of the soul that can operate apart from a body postmortem. I extended that idea to apply to persons whose brains are undeveloped, injured, or malformed in one way or another, and I argued that just as the intellective soul is able to know and love God postmortem with God's support, so also can those with cognitive impairment know and love God in this life with God's support. In other words, they can live toward their created *telos* of being in relationship with God. When understood in this way, all humans not only are the image of God, but are able to function as such.

Finally, I argued that humans are worshipping beings, created for the purpose of worshipping the one true God—both giving him glory and reflecting his glory to the world. As worshipping beings, humans direct their worship either to God or to something other than God. Where their worship is directed affects whether humans are becoming more like God, as he intended from their creation in his image, or more like something else. As Beale writes, we become what we revere. In summary, this chapter has argued that all humans are material-spiritual, intellective, worshipping animals who are becoming either like God as he intended—or like the idols they revere.

Conclusion

MY PURPOSE IN THIS book was to demonstrate that although humans are a type of animal, as modern science asserts, they are more than that. When considered biblically, scientifically, and theologically, humans are specially unique and differ from other created physical beings not just in degree but in kind. In this concluding chapter, I will review the arguments I have offered throughout the book and offer some implications of my contention that humans are specially unique.

We began by considering Aquinas, a premodern exegete and theologian whose description of humans in the *Summa Theologiae* recognizes them as both like and unlike other creatures, an assertion that centers on the biblical teaching that humans are not just like other creatures as material-spiritual beings but also like God as intellective beings. We then explored a number of biblical texts, including the creation accounts in Genesis. I argued that Scripture—a key source for Aquinas—portrays humans as specially unique beings as well. Humans are not only the image of God with all that entails, but they are also teleological beings created to be in a personal relationship with God, one characterized by knowing and loving him.

Moving to science, I argued that while it is controversial to assert that humans are specially unique with respect to other creatures, given the available evidence, especially from our nearest genetic relatives (the chimpanzees), that assertion is defensible. We then digressed a bit to consider how to understand apparent contradictions between what we learn about humans from Scripture and what we learn from science. I argued, given the priority of Scripture as the ultimate authority for faith and life, that we should consider these sources as two stories that need not be harmonized. From a pastoral perspective, this allows for a level of epistemic comfortability for many people. If we agree that humans are portrayed as specially unique in Scripture in the ways I have described, the best posture for many people is to live with any apparent tension between the story of science and the story of Scripture as mystery or paradox, a category not unknown in the tradition of the church. Finally, using the evidence gleaned from all of these sources, I proposed that we consider humans specially unique because we are spiritual-material, intellective, worshipping beings, whose created *telos* is to know and love God.

So why does this matter? What are some implications from this assertion? I am a theologian whose primary work is to serve the church both in my teaching and in my writing. The primary implications of this project, therefore, are pastoral. These implications have already been hinted at in previous chapters, but it would be helpful to review and perhaps expand them just a bit here. While a retrieval of Aquinas has been helpful for framing the theological constructions throughout my argument, in this section I will turn to my confessional roots to guide my thinking, relying on the very pastoral sixteenth-century confession, the Heidelberg Catechism.

Human dignity is the first implication of human special uniqueness as I have defined it. The *Oxford English Dictionary* defines dignity as "the quality of being worthy or honorable; worthiness, worth, nobleness, excellence."[1] Interpreting a number of biblical texts, the sixth question and answer of the Heidelberg Catechism says of humans: "God created them good and in his own image, that is, in true righteousness and holiness, so that they might truly know God their creator, love him with all their heart, and live with him in eternal happiness for his praise and glory."[2] To be made like God for the *telos* of a personal relationship with God bestows incredible honor. But perhaps even greater honor is given to humans in the incarnation, where God lowers himself to take on human nature for the purpose of restoring humans to their *telos* of relationship with God. In *Evangelium Vitae*, his encyclical on the value of human life, Pope John Paul II writes that Christ's incarnation "reveals to humanity not only the boundless love of God who 'so loved the world that he gave his only Son' (John 3:16), but also the incomparable value of every human person."[3] What greater honor could there be than for God to become like us so that we could become like him, just as he intended?

Recognizing the dignity of all humans as taught by Scripture means that the church must be on the front lines defending the dignity of all

1. *Oxford English Dictionary*, s.v. "dignity."
2. Heidelberg Catechism 6.
3. John Paul II, *Evangelium Vitae*, 2.

people, especially the voiceless ones at the edges of life. John Paul II offers a partial list of actions that undermine human dignity. He writes:

> Whatever is opposed to life itself, such as any type of murder, genocide, abortion, euthanasia, or willful self-destruction, whatever violates the integrity of the human person, such as mutilation, torments inflicted on body or mind, attempts to coerce the will itself; whatever insults human dignity, such as subhuman living conditions, arbitrary imprisonment, deportation, slavery, prostitution, the selling of women and children; as well as disgraceful working conditions, where people are treated as mere instruments of gain rather than as free and responsible persons; all these things and others like them are infamies indeed.[4]

Affirmation of human dignity, a dignity not shared by other animals, militates against these offenses. Proper rule of creation entails care for all things living and nonliving. Human dignity raises the bar of creation care to neighbor love, the second great commandment. The Heidelberg Catechism tells us that the "second table of the law[5] . . . teaches us what we owe our neighbor."[6] The exposition of each of these commandments not only tells us what we must *not* do, but what we *must* do to protect and guard our neighbor. Human dignity requires that the church fight against suggestions that any human or group of humans does not have the infinite worth of being made in the image of their Creator and therefore does not deserve to be protected and guarded. Advocacy on issues concerning social justice like those listed by John Paul II are not an optional add-on to the gospel; it is the outworking of the gospel itself.[7] Indeed, the inherent worth of all humans calls Christians proactively to care for their neighbors, as the Heidelberg Catechism suggests—most especially neighbors at the edges of life who are unable to care for or advocate for themselves.

The second implication of my thesis that humans are specially unique as material-spiritual, intellective, worshipping beings is the assurance of continued fellowship with Christ despite profound disability, as argued in chapter 5, or death as I will suggest here. While all Christians affirm the

---

4. John Paul II, *Evangelium Vitae*, 3.

5. Honor your father and mother, do not murder, do not commit adultery, do not steal, do not bear false witness, and do not covet.

6. Heidelberg Catechism 93.

7. For a wonderful description of this outworking of the gospel, see Billings, *Union with Christ*.

resurrection of the body as the final state, the intermediate state—the time between death and the final resurrection—has begun to fall on hard times in some academic circles. Nonetheless, I suggest that for the vast majority of people in the pews or chairs of our churches, the idea that their loved one is *not* with the Lord would be disturbing. "Where is my wife, my husband, my parent, my child?" people ask after experiencing the death of a loved one. Due to the understanding that humans are material-spiritual beings, the church's answer has traditionally been "with the Lord and the souls of the faithful." The Heidelberg Catechism articulates this basic understanding of the church in its teaching that death "puts an end to our sinning and is our entrance to eternal life."[8] The Heidelberg Catechism, in keeping with the historic teaching of the church in no way suggests a gap between physical death and the final resurrection.

As material-spiritual beings, those who die in Christ are still alive with Christ during this temporary separation of body and soul. They await the resurrection and final judgment with him while experiencing a foretaste of glory even now. Our only comfort, in life and in death, as the Heidelberg Catechism's first question and answer states, is that we belong body and soul in life *and* in death to our faithful savior Jesus Christ. Our loved ones are away from the body, in that time between the times, but we can rest in the assurance that they are at home with their Lord and we can assure those who have lost someone dear that this is the case.

The third implication of affirming humans as specially unique, particularly as worshipping beings, is that who or what we worship matters. I think that most Christians know this. It's just not clear that this basic orthodoxy shapes our orthopraxy, perhaps especially in the Western church. Twenty-five years ago, theologian Donald McCullough raised the question of whom the Western church worships, suggesting that we have trivialized God, preferring various gods of our own making to the one true God revealed in Scripture.[9] Many of the gods McCullough identified continue to plague the church. The problem with all of the gods he identified, as well as many more that have arisen since then, is that while they may resemble the one true God, they are really about not listening to what God may demand of us, but rather making clear our demands on God. These are gods that serve us on *our* terms, not the God that we serve on his terms.

---

8. Heidelberg Catechism 42.
9. McCullough, *Trivialization of God*, 13–26.

The Heidelberg Catechism defines idolatry as "having or inventing something in which one trusts in place of or alongside of the only true God, who has revealed himself in his Word."[10] When we allow ourselves to trust in our experience or favorite cause or identity or comfort or success or anything else, even at the same level that we trust in God, these things have become our idols, and as we worship these or other cultural idols, we begin to conform to their standards rather than God's. Instead of conforming to the image of Christ (Rom 8:29), who is both the source and exemplar of true human existence, cultural idols point us away from our true humanity, conforming us instead to something of our own making. Jared Ortiz writes in his discussion of Augustine's understanding of creation, "The rational creature who chooses lesser things becomes less himself."[11] In short, insofar as we worship something other than God as he has revealed himself, we become less human. And as G. K. Beale writes, "We resemble what we revere, either for ruin or restoration."[12]

If this sounds a bit grim, it is because I think idolatry is one of the most pressing issues for the Western church, particularly the church in the United States. The gods of consumerism, politics, identity, causes—just or otherwise—all vie for our loyalty. The church appears more and more loathe to accept reality as God has defined it. We want to define our own reality, including the reality of God himself. Instead of the God who left people trembling on the edges of Mt. Sinai and at Calvary, the church prefers a god of love loosely defined as whatever affirms our choices and makes us happy. Idolatry is dangerous, as people like McCullough and Beale point out. It leads to destruction. While it may provide temporary happiness, it can never provide the lasting comfort that a personal relationship with the one true God provides.

The Heidelberg Catechism provides a beautiful description of this comfort that comes from our Creator, who reaches out with grace to all who will hear but at the same time demands to be known, loved, and worshipped on his terms.

> *What is your only comfort in life and in death?*
> That I am not my own, but belong—body and soul, in life and in death—to my faithful Savior Jesus Christ. He has fully paid for all my sins with his precious blood, and has set me free from the

10. Heidelberg Catechism 95.
11. Ortiz, *"You Made Us for Yourself,"* 34–35.
12. Beale, *We Become What We Worship*, 49.

tyranny of the devil. He also watches over me in such a way that not a hair can fall from my head without the will of my Father in heaven: in fact, all things must work together for my salvation. Because I belong to him, Christ, by his Holy Spirit, assures me of eternal life and makes me wholeheartedly willing and ready from now on to live for him. (The Heidelberg Catechism, Q. and A. 1)

In an age of so many false gods that promise much but can deliver nothing, this document's first statement reminds its readers where comfort really lies—in belonging to the God who in Christ and by his Holy Spirit makes possible an interpersonal relationship with him not just in this life, but forever.

Bibliography

Adler, Margo. "The Chimp That Learned Sign Language." *Day to Day*, May 28, 2008. NPR. https://www.npr.org/2008/05/28/90516132/the-chimp-that-learned-sign-language.

Alter, Robert. *Genesis: Translation and Commentary.* New York: Norton, 1996.

American Psychological Association. "Empathy." *APA Dictionary of Psychology.* https://dictionary.apa.org/empathy/.

Andersen, Bernhard W. *From Creation to New Creation.* Minneapolis: Fortress, 1994.

Aquinas, Thomas. *Summa Theologica.* https://ccel.org/ccel/aquinas/summa/summa.

Alexander, Denis. *Is There Purpose in Biology? The Cost of Existence and the God of Love.* Oxford: Lion House, 2018.

Arnold, Bill. "Necromancy and Cleromancy in 1 and 2 Samuel." *Catholic Biblical Quarterly* 66, no. 2 (2004) 199–213.

Ayala, Francisco. "Biology Precedes, Culture Transcends: An Evolutionist's View of Human Nature." *Zygon* 33, no. 4 (1998) 507–23.

Barrett, Justin L., and Matthew J. Jarvinen. "Cognitive Evolution, Human Uniqueness, and the *Imago Dei*." In *Emergence of Personhood*, edited by Malcolm Jeeves, 163–83. Grand Rapids: Eerdmans, 2015.

Barth, Karl. *Church Dogmatics* 3/1, *The Doctrine of Creation.* Edited by G. W. Bromiley and T. F. Torrance. Edinburgh: T. & T. Clark, 1960.

Bauckham, Richard. *Living with Other Creatures: Green Exegesis and Theology.* Waco, TX: Baylor University Press, 2011.

Bauerschmidt, Frederick Christian. "Reading the *Summa Theologiae*." In *Cambridge Companion to the Summa Theologiae*, edited by Philip McCosker and Denys Turner, 9–22. Cambridge: Cambridge University Press, 2016.

Bauks, Micaela. "'Soul Concepts' in Ancient Near Eastern Mythical Texts and Their Implications for the Primeval History." *Vetus Testamentum* 66, no. 2 (2016) 181–93.

Bavinck, Herman. *Reformed Dogmatics*, vol. 4, *Holy Spirit, Church, and New Creation.* Edited by John Bolt. Translated by John Vriend. Grand Rapids: Baker Academic, 2008.

Bazán, B. Carlos. "The Human Soul: Form and Substance? Thomas Aquinas' Critique of Eclectic Aritotelianism." *Archives d'histoire doctrinale et littéraire du Moyen Age* 64 (1997), 95–126.

Beale, G. K. *We Become What We Worship: A Biblical Theology of Idolatry.* Downers Grove, IL: IVP Academic, 2008.

Bekoff, Marc, and Alan Colin. "Deep Ethology, Animal Rights, and the Great Ape/Animal Project: Resisting Speciesism and Expanding the Community of Equals." *Journal of Agricultural and Environmental Ethics* 10 (1997) 269–96.

Bergman, Joshua A. *Inconsistency in the Torah: Ancient Literary Convention and the Limits of Source Criticism.* Oxford: Oxford University Press, 2017.

Billings, J. Todd. *Union with Christ: Reframing Theology and Ministry for the Church.* Grand Rapids: Baker Academic, 2011.

Bird, Phyllis. "'Male and Female He Created Them': Gen. 1:27b in the Context of the Priestly Account of Creation." *Harvard Theological Review* 74, no. 2 (1981) 129–59.

Bloom, Paul. *Descartes' Baby: How the Science of Child Development Explains What Makes Us Human.* New York: Basic, 2004.

Bolt, John. "The Relation between Creation and Redemption in Romans 8:18–27." *Calvin Theological Journal* 30, no. 1 (1995) 34–51.

Brown, Francis, S. R. Driver, and Charles A. Briggs. *Hebrew and English Lexicon.* 2nd ed. Peabody, MA: Hendrikson, 1996.

Brownson, James. *The Bible, Gender, and Sexuality: Reframing the Church's Debate on Same-sex Relationships.* Grand Rapids: Eerdmans, 2013.

Brubacher, John. "Not Just Another Animal: Evolution and Human Distinctiveness." *Vision: A Journal for Church and Theology* 20, no. 1 (2019) 21–28.

Brubacher, John. "Not Just Another Animal: Evolution and Human Distinctiveness." *Vision* 20, no. 1 (2019) 21–28.

Brueggemann, Walter. "Exodus." In *The New Interpreter's Bible* 1, edited by Leander E. Keck, 677–981. Nashville: Abingdon, 1994.

———. *Genesis.* Interpretation. Louisville: Westminster John Knox, 2005.

———. *Theology of the Old Testament: Testimony, Dispute, Advocacy.* Minneapolis: Fortress, 1997.

Byrne, Richard W. "The Dividing Line: What Sets Humans Apart from Our Closest Relatives?" In *Emergence of Personhood*, edited by Malcolm Jeeves, 13–36. Grand Rapids: Eerdmans, 2015.

Calvin, John. *Commentary on the Book of Psalms.* Translated by James Anderson. Edinburgh: Edinburgh Printing Company, 1845.

Cantor, Carla. "Project Nim Revisited." *Columbia News*, October 11, 2019. https://news.columbia.edu/news/chimpanzee-language-project-nim-herbert-terrace/.

Clump, Barbara C., Matthew Cantat, and Christian Rutz. "Raw-material Selectivity in Hook-tool-crafting New Caledonian Crows." *Biology Letters* 15, no. 2 (2019) 1–6.

Collins, John C. *Reading Genesis Well: Navigating History, Poetry, Science, and Truth in Genesis 1–11.* Grand Rapids: Zondervan, 2018.

Cook, L. M., et al. "Selective Bird Predation on the Peppered Moth: The Last Experiment of Michael Majerus." *Biology Letters* 8, no. 4 (2012) 609–12.

Cooper, John W. *Body, Soul, and Life Everlasting: Biblical Anthropology and the Monism-Dualism Debate.* Grand Rapids: Eerdmans, 1989.

———. "Scripture and Philosophy on the Unity of Body and Soul: An Integrative Method for Theological Anthropology." In *Ashgate Research Companion to Theological Anthropology*, edited by Joshua Farris and Charles Taliaferro, 27–42. Farnham, UK: Ashgate, 2015.

Corcoran, Kevin. *Rethinking Human Nature: A Christian Materialist Alternative to the Soul.* Grand Rapids: Baker Academic, 2006.

Cortez, Marc. *Theological Anthropology: A Guide for the Perplexed.* London: T. & T. Clark, 2010.

———. *Theological Anthropology in Historical Perspective: Ancient and Contemporary Approaches to Theological Anthropology.* Grand Rapids: Zondervan, 2016.

Cunningham, David S. "The Way of All Flesh: Re-thinking the *Imago Dei.*" In *Creaturely Theology: On God, Humans, and Other Animals,* edited by Celia Deane-Drummond and David Clough, 100–117. London: SCM, 2009.

Davies, Brian. *Thomas Aquinas's Summa Theologiae: A Guide and Commentary.* Oxford: Oxford University Press, 2014.

———. *The Thought of Thomas Aquinas.* Oxford: Oxford University Press, 1992.

Dawkins, Richard. *The Greatest Show on Earth: The Evidence for Evolution.* New York: Free, 2009.

———. *River Out of Eden: A Darwinian View of Life.* New York: Basic, 1995.

Dennett, Daniel C. *Darwin's Dangerous Idea: Evolution and the Meanings of Life.* New York: Simon and Schuster, 1995.

Deroche, Michael. "Isaiah XLV 7 and the Creation of Chaos." *Vetus Testamentum* 42, no. 1 (1992) 11–21.

DeYoung, Rebecca Konyndyk, Colleen McCloskey and Christina Van Dyke. *Aquinas's Ethics: Metaphysical Foundations, Moral Theory, and Theological Context.* Notre Dame, IN: University of Notre Dame Press, 2009.

De Waal, Frans. *Good Natured: The Origins of Right and Wrong in Humans and Other Animals.* Cambridge, MA: Harvard University Press, 1997.

———. "Natural Normativity: The 'Is' and 'Ought' of Animal Behavior." *Behavior* 151 (2014) 185–204.

———. *Peacemaking among Primates.* Cambridge: Harvard University Press, 1990.

Dunstan, Sylvia. "Lord, You Are Both Lamb and Shepherd." © GIA, 1991.

Durham, John I. *Exodus.* Word Biblical Commentary 3. Waco, TX: Word, 1987.

Farris, Joshua R. *An Introduction to Theological Anthropology.* Grand Rapids: Baker Academic, 2020.

Farris, Joshua A., and Charles Taliaferro, eds. *The Ashgate Research Companion to Theological Anthropology.* Farnham, Surrey, UK: Ashgate, 2015.

Fletcher-Louis, Crispin H. T. "God's Image, His Cosmic Temple and the High Priest: Towards an Historical and Theological Account of the Incarnation." In *Heaven on Earth: The Temple in Biblical Theology,* edited by T. Desmond Alexander and Simon J. Gathercole, 81–100. Carlisle, UK: Paternoster, 2004.

Fox, Everett. *The Five Books of Moses: A New Translation with Introductions, Commentary, and Notes.* The Schocken Bible 1. New York: Schocken, 1983.

Freeman, Anthony. "Editorial Introduction." *Modern Believing* 57.2 (2016) 115–17

Fretheim, Terence. *God and the World in the Old Testament: A Relational Theolog.y of Creation.* Nashville: Abingdon, 2005.

———. *The Pentateuch.* Nashville: Abingdon, 1996.

Fridovich-Keil, Judith L. "Human Genome." *Britannica.* https://www.britannica.com/science/human-genome/.

Gibbons, Ann. "Bonobos Join Chimps as Closest Human Relatives." *Science,* June 13, 2012. https://www.sciencemag.org/news/2012/06/bonobos-join-chimps-closest-human-relatives/.

Gilson, Etienne. *The Christian Philosophy of St. Thomas Aquinas.* New York: Random House, 1956.

Gingrich, F. Wilbur, and Frederick W. Danker. *A Greek-English Lexicon of the New Testament and Other Early Christian Literature*. Chicago: University of Chicago Press, 1979.

Grenz, Stanley. *The Social God and the Relational Self: A Trinitarian Theology of the Imago Dei*. Louisville, KY: Westminster John Knox, 2001.

Goetz, Stewart. "Substance Dualism." In *Ashgate Research Companion to Theological Anthropology*, edited by Farris and Taliaferro, 125–38. Farnham, UK: Ashgate, 2015.

Green, Joel B. *Body, Soul, and Human Life: The Nature of Humanity in the Bible*. Grand Rapids: Baker Academic, 2008.

Green, Joel B., and Stuart L. Palmer, eds. *Rethinking Human Nature: A Christian Materialist Alternative to the Soul*. Grand Rapids: Baker Academic, 2006.

Gunkel, Hermann. "The Influence of Babylonian Mythology upon The Biblical Creation Story." In *Creation in the Old Testament*, edited by Bernhard W. Anderson, translated by Charles A. Muenchow, 25–52. Philadelphia: Fortress, 1984.

Hare, Brian, Josep Call, and Michael Tomasello. "Do Chimpanzees Know What Conspecifics Know?" *Animal Behavior* 61, no. 1 (2001) 139–51.

Herring, Stephen L. "A 'Transubstantiated' Humanity: The Relationship between the Divine Image and the Presence of God in Genesis I 26f." *Vetus Testamentum* 58 (2008) 480–94.

Herzfeld, Noreen L. *In Our Image: Artificial Intelligence and the Human Spirit*. Minneapolis: Fortress, 2002.

Hoekema, Anthony A. *Created in God's Image*. Grand Rapids: Eerdmans, 1986.

Horton, Michael. *The Christian Faith: A Systematic Theology for Pilgrims on the Way*. Grand Rapids: Zondervan, 2011.

"How Should We Interpret the Bible?" Biologos. https://biologos.org/common-questions/how-should-we-interpret-the-bible/.

Jaki, Stanley L. *Genesis 1 through the Ages*. London: Moore, 1992.

Jeeves, Malcolm, ed. *The Emergence of Personhood: A Quantum Leap*. Grand Rapids: Eerdmans, 2015.

Jenkins, Philip. *The New Faces of Christianity: Believing the Bible in the Global South*. Oxford: Oxford University Press, 2003.

John Paul II, Pope. *Evangelium Vitae*. Encyclical on the Value and Inviolability of Human Life. March 25, 1995.

Kärkkäinen, Veli-Matti. *Creation and Humanity*. A Constructive Christian Theology for the Pluralistic World 3. Grand Rapids: Eerdmans, 2015.

Kerr-Gafney, Jess, et al. "Cognitive and Affective Empathy in Eating Disorders: A Systematic Review and Meta-Analysis." *Frontiers in Psychiatry* 10 (2019) 102. https://www.ncbi.nlm.nih.gov/pmc/articles/PMC6410675/.

Knight, Douglas A. "Cosmogony and Order in the Hebrew Tradition." In *Cosmogony and Ethical Order: New Studies in Comparative Ethics*, edited by Robin W. Lovin and Frank E. Reynolds, 133–57. Chicago: University of Chicago Press, 1985.

Kretzman, Norman. *The Metaphysics of Creation: Aquinas's Natural Theology in Summa Contra Gentiles II*. Oxford: Clarendon, 1999.

Krupenye, Christopher, Fumihiro Kano, Satoshi Hirata, Josep Call, and Michael Tomasello. "Great Apes Anticipate That Other Individuals Will Act According to False Beliefs." *Science* 354, no. 6308 (2016) 110–14.

LaCugna, Catherine. *God for Us: The Trinity and Christian Life*. San Francisco: Harper San Francisco, 1992.

Lambdin, Thomas O. *Introduction to Biblical Hebrew*. New York: Scribner's Sons, 1971.

Levering, Matthew. *Engaging the Doctrine of Creation: Cosmos, Creatures, and the Wise and Good Creator*. Grand Rapids: Baker Academic, 2017.

———. *Scripture and Metaphysics: Aquinas and the Renewal of Trinitarian Theology*. Malden, MA: Blackwell, 2004.

Levin, Harold. *The Earth through Time*. 9th ed. Hoboken: John Wiley, 2010.

Linzey, Andrew. *Christianity and the Rights of Animals*. New York: Crossroad, 1987.

———. "The Theological Basis of Animal Rights." *Christian Century*, October 9, 1991, 906–9.

Livingstone, David N. *Adam's Ancestors: Race, Religion, and the Politics of Human Origins*. Baltimore: Johns Hopkins University Press, 2008.

Lowry, Mark. "Mary Did You Know." © Word Music, 1991.

MacIntyre, Alasdair. *Dependent, Rational, Animals: Why Human Beings Need the Virtues*. Chicago: Open Court, 1999.

Madueme, Hans. "From Sin to the Soul: A Dogmatic Argument for Dualism." In *The Christian Doctrine of Humanity: Explorations in Constructive Dogmatics,* edited by Oliver D. Crisp and Fred Sanders, 70–90. Grand Rapids: Zondervan, 2018.

Max, D. T. "Beyond Human." *National Geographic*, Spring 2017, 40–63.

McCall, Thomas. *Against God and Nature*. Wheaton, IL: Crossway, 2019.

McCosker, Philip, and Denys Turner, eds. *The Cambridge Companion to the Summa Theologiae*. Cambridge: Cambridge University Press, 2016.

McCullough, Donald C. *The Trivialization of God: The Dangerous Illusion of a Manageable Deity*. Colorado Springs: NavPress, 1995.

McFarlane, Keri. "Living Relationally with Creation: Animals and the Christian Faith." *Perspectives on Science and Christian Faith* 67, no. 4 (2015) 235–44.

McGrath, Alister E. *Dawkins' God: From The Selfish Gene to The God Delusion*. Chichester, UK: Wiley-Blackwell, 2015.

Merricks, Trenton. "The Resurrection of the Body and the Life Everlasting." In *Reason for the Hope Within*, edited by Michael Murray, 261–86. Grand Rapids: Eerdmans, 1999.

Middleton, J. Richard. *The Liberating Image: The Imago Dei in Genesis 1*. Grand Rapids: Brazos, 2005.

Milgrom, Jacob. *Leviticus 17–22: A New Translation with Introduction and Commentary*. Anchor Bible 3A. New York: Doubleday, 2000.

Miller, Robert D., II. "The Hebrew Bible's Concept of Life." *Communio Viatorum* 57, no. 3 (2015) 223–39.

Mora-Bermudez, Felipe, Farhath Badsha, Sabina Kanton, et al. "Differences and Similarities between Human and Chimpanzee Neural Progenitors during Cerebral Cortex Development." *eLife*, September 26, 2016. https://elifesciences.org/articles/18683/.

Moreland, J. P., and Scott B. Rae. *Body and Soul: Human Nature and the Crisis in Ethics*. Downers Grove, IL: IVP Academic, 2000.

Moritz, Joshua. "Human Uniqueness, the Other Hominids, and 'Anthropocentrism of the Gaps' in the Religion and Science Dialogue." *Zygon* 47, no. 1 (2012) 65–96.

Morris, Henry. *The Remarkable Birth of Planet Earth*. Minneapolis: Dimension, 1972.

Müller, Richard A. "Reading Aquinas from a Reformed Perspective: A Review Essay." *Calvin Theological Journal* 53, no. 2 (2018) 255–88.

Murphy, Nancey. *Bodies and Souls, or Spirited Bodies*. Cambridge: Cambridge University Press, 2006.

——. "Nonreductive Physicalism." In *In Search of the Soul: Four Views of the Mind-Body Problem*, edited by Joel B. Green and Stuart L. Palmer, 115–37. Downers Grove, IL: IVP Academic, 2005.

National Library of Medicine. "What Is Noncoding DNA?" *MedlinePlus*. https://medlineplus.gov/genetics/understanding/basics/noncodingdna/.

Niditch, Susan. *Chaos to Cosmos: Studies in Biblical Patterns of Creation*. Scholars Press Studies in the Humanities. Chico, CA: Scholars, 1985.

Niskanen, Paul. "The Poetics of Adam: The Creation of םדא in the Image of םיהלא." *Journal of Biblical Literature* 128, no. 3 (2009) 417–36.

Norris, Jeffrey. "What Makes Us Human? Studies of Chimp and Human DNA May Tell Us." University of California San Francisco, June 28, 2010. https://www.ucsf.edu/news/2010/06/5993/what-makes-us-human-studies-chimp-and-human-dna-may-tell-us/.

Nürnberger, Klaus. "The Conquest of Chaos: The Biblical Paradigm of Creation and Its Contemporary Relevance." *Journal of Theology for Southern Africa* 98 (1997) 45–63.

O'Callaghan, John P. "*Imago Dei*: A Test Case for St. Thomas's Augustinianism." In *Aquinas the Augustinian*, edited by Michael Dauphinais, Barry David, and Matthew Levering, 100–144. Washington, DC: Catholic University of America Press, 2007.

O'Donovan, Oliver. *Resurrection and Moral Order: An Outline for an Evangelical Ethics*. Leicester, UK: InterVarsity, 1986.

Oliphant, K. Scott. *Thomas Aquinas*. Phillipsburg, NJ: P&R, 2017.

O'Neil, Dennis. "Humans." *Primates: The Taxonomy and General Characteristics of Prosimians, Monkeys, Apes, and Humans*. https://www2.palomar.edu/anthro/primate/prim_8.htm.

Ortiz, Jared. *"You Made Us for Yourself": Creation in St. Augustine's* Confessions. Minneapolis: Fortress, 2016.

Oswalt, John. *The Book of Isaiah: Chapters 1–39*, New International Commentary on the Old Testament. Grand Rapids: Eerdmans, 1986.

Otzen, Benedict. "דבל." In *Theological Dictionary of the Old Testament* 2, edited by G. Johannes Botterweck. Rev. ed. Grand Rapids: Eerdmans, 1977.

Pardee, Dennis. "A New Aramaic Inscription from Zincirli." *Bulletin of the American Schools of Oriental Research* 356 (2009) 51–71.

Parsenios, George L. "The Orthodox Paradox." Greek Orthodox Archdiocese of America. https://www.goarch.org/-/the-orthodox-paradox/.

Payton, James R. *Light from the Christian East: An Introduction to the Orthodox Tradition*. Downers Grove, IL: IVP Academic, 2007.

Plantinga, Alvin. *Knowledge and Christian Belief*. Grand Rapids: Eerdmans, 2015.

Plantinga, Cornelius, Jr, "Deep Wisdom." In *God the Holy Trinity: Reflections of Christian Faith and Practice,* edited by Timothy George, 149–56. Grand Rapids: Baker Academic, 2006.

——. "Images of God." In *Christian Faith and Practice in the Modern World: Theology from an Evangelical Point of View*, edited by Mark A. Noll and David F. Wells, 51–67. Grand Rapids: Eerdmans, 1988.

Pleijel, Richard. "To Be or to Have a *Nephesh*: Gen. 2:7 and the Irresistible Tide of Monism." *Zeitschrift für die alttestamentliche Wissenschaft* 131, no. 2 (2019) 194–206.

——. "Translating the Biblical Hebrew Word *Nephesh* in Light of New Research." *Bible Translator* 70, no. 2 (2019) 154–66.

Post, Stephen G. "A Moral Case for Nonreductive Physicalism." In *Whatever Happened to the Soul: Scientific and Theological Portraits of Human Nature,* edited by Warren S. Brown, Nancey Murphy, and H. Newton Maloney, 195–212. Minneapolis: Fortress, 1998.

Pressler, Carolyn. "Certainty, Ambiguity, and Trust: Knowledge of God in Psalm 139." In *A God So Near: Essays in Honor of Patrick Miller,* edited by. Brett A. Strawn and Nancy R. Bowen, 91–100. Winona Lake, IN: Eisenbrauns, 2003.

Propp, William H. C. *Exodus 19–40: A New Translation and Commentary.* Anchor Bible 2A. New York: Doubleday, 2006.

Putz, Oliver. "Moral Apes, Human Uniqueness, and the Image of God." *Zygon* 44, no. 3 (2009) 613–24.

Regan, Tom. "The Moral Basis of Vegetarianism." *Canadian Journal of Philosophy* 5, no. 2 (1975) 181–214.

Reinders, Han S. *Receiving the Gift of Friendship: Profound Disability, Theological Anthropology, and Ethics.* Grand Rapids: Eerdmans, 2008.

Reno, R. R. *Genesis.* Brazos Theological Commentary on the Bible. Grand Rapids: Brazos, 2010.

Sefina, Carl. "The Depths of Animal Grief." *Nova,* July 8, 2015. https://www.pbs.org/wgbh/nova/article/animal-grief/.

Shuster, Marguerite. "Who Are We?" In *Who We Are: Our Dignity as Human: A Neo-Evangelical Theology,* edited by Paul K. Jewett and Marguerite Shuster, 11–16. Grand Rapids: Eerdmans, 1996.

Singer, Peter. *In Defense of Animals.* Oxford: Blackwell, 1985.

Siri, Giuseppe. "Death and the Immensity That Awaits Us." *Inside the Vatican.* https://insidethevatican.com/magazine/culture/death-and-the-immensity-that-awaits-us-a-reflection-on-eternity-and-heaven/.

Smith, Christian. *Moral, Believing Animals: Human Personhood and Culture.* Oxford: Oxford University Press, 2003.

Sonderegger, Katherine. *Systematic Theology,* Vol. 1, *The Doctrine of God.* Minneapolis: Fortress, 2015.

Speiser, E. A. *Genesis.* Anchor Bible 1. Garden City, NY: Doubleday, 1964.

Stearley, Ralph. "Assessing Evidences for the Evolution of a Human Cognitive Platform for 'Soulish Behaviors.'" *Perspectives in Science and the Christian Faith* 61, no. 3 (2009) 152–74.

Steiner, Richard. *Disembodied Souls: The Nephesh in Israel and Kindred Spirits in the Ancient Near East, with an Appendix on the Katumuwa Inscription.* Atlanta: Society of Biblical Literature, 2015.

Stump, Eleonore. *Aquinas.* London: Routledge, 2003.

Stump, Jim. "Scientific Testimonies to Human Uniqueness." *BioLogos* (blog). May 21, 2018. https://biologos.org/post/scientific-testimonies-to-human-uniqueness/.

Suddendorf, Thomas. *The Gap: The Science of What Separates Us from Other Animals.* New York: Basic, 2013.

Swinton, John. *Dementia: Living in the Memories of God.* Grand Rapids: Eerdmans, 2012.

Tattersall, Ian. *Paleontology: A Brief History of Life.* Radnor, PA: Templeton, 2010.

Tennant, Timothy C. *Theology in the Context of World Christianity: How the Global Church Is Influencing the Way We Think about and Discuss Theology.* Grand Rapids: Zondervan, 2007.

Torrell, Jean-Pierre. *Aquinas's Summa: Background, Structure, and Reception*. Washington, DC: Catholic University of America Press, 2005.

Treier. Daniel J. *Introducing Theological Interpretation of Scripture: Recovering a Christian Practice*. Grand Rapids: Baker Academic, 2008.

Trible, Phyllis. *God and the Rhetoric of Sexuality*. Philadelphia: Fortress, 1978.

Turner, Denys. "The Human Person." In *Cambridge Companion to the Summa Theologiae*, edited by McCosker and Turner, 168–80.

Van Dam, Cornelius. "לדך." In *New International Dictionary of Old Testament Theology and Exegesis*, vol. 1, rev. ed., edited by Willem VanGemeren, 603–5. Grand Rapids: Zondervan, 1997.

Vanden Berg, Mary L. "Christ's Atonement: The Hope of Creation." PhD diss., Calvin Theological Seminary, 2008.

———. "The Impact of a Gap in Existence on Christology and Soteriology: A Challenge for Physicalists." *Calvin Theological Journal* 49, no. 2 (2014) 248–57.

Van den Brink, Gijsbert, *Reformed Theology and Evolutionary Theory*. Grand Rapids: Eerdmans, 2020.

Van der Kooi, Cornelius, and Gijsbert van den Brink. *Christian Dogmatics: An Introduction*. Translated by Reinder Bruinsma with James D. Bratt. Grand Rapids: Eerdmans, 2017.

Van Huyssteen, J. Wentzel. *Alone in the World? Human Uniqueness in Science and Theology*. Grand Rapids: Eerdmans, 2006.

Valkenberg, Pim. "Scripture." In *Cambridge Companion to the Summa Theologiae*, edited by Philip McCosker and Denys Turner, 48–61. Cambridge: Cambridge University Press, 2016.

Viazovski, Yaroslav. *Image and Hope: John Calvin and Karl Barth on Body, Soul, and Life Everlasting*. Eugene, OR: Pickwick, 2015.

Waltke, Bruce. "The Literary Genre of Genesis Chapter One." *Crux* 27 (1991) 2–10.

Walton, John H. *Genesis 1 as Ancient Cosmology*. University Park, PA: Penn State University Press, 2011.

———. *Genesis*. NIV Application Commentary. Grand Rapids: Zondervan, 2001.

Wilcox, David L. "Our Genetic Prehistory: Did Our Genes Make Us Human?" *Perspectives on Science and the Christian Faith* 66, no. 2 (2014) 83–94.

Wenham, Gordon J. *Genesis 1–15*. Word Biblical Commentary 1. Waco, TX: Word, 1987.

Wernick, Adam. "Sweating Is an Essential and Uniquely Human Function." *The World*. Science Friday. August 28, 2017. https://www.pri.org/stories/2017-08-28/sweating-essential-and-uniquely-human-function/.

Westermann, Claus. *Genesis 1–11*. Continental Commentaries. Minneapolis: Augsburg, 1984.

Whitekettle, Richard. "Marriage Equality and the Bible: Why All Forms of Marriage in the Old Testament Are Not Equal." *Public Discourse: The Journal of the Witherspoon Institute*. May 12, 2014. https://www.thepublicdiscourse.com/2014/05/13054/.

Whybray, R. N. *The Making of the Pentateuch: A Methodological Study*. Journal for the Study of the Old Testament Supplement Series 53. Sheffield, UK: JSOT, 1987.

Witvliet, John D. "The Trinitarian DNA of Christian Worship: Perennial Themes in Recent Theological Literature." *Colloquium* 2 (2005). https://dev.ism.yale.edu/publications/colloquium-journal/autumn-2005/.

Wolchover, Natalie. "Chimps vs. Humans: How Are We Different?" *Live Science*, July 29, 2011. https://www.livescience.com/15297-chimps-humans.html.

Wright, N. T. "The Big Picture: The New Testament and the Mission of God." Public lecture presented at Calvin College, Grand Rapids, November 20, 2013.

———. *The New Testament in Its World: An Introduction to the History, Literature, and Theology of the First Christians*. Grand Rapids: Zondervan, 2019.

———. "The Letter to the Romans: Introduction, Commentary, and Reflections." In *The New Interpreter's Bible* 10, edited by Leander E. Keck, William L. Lane, and Marion L. Soards, 395–770. Nashville: Abingdon, 2002.

Young, Davis A. "Christianity and the Age of the Earth." In *Is God a Creationist?* edited by Roland Mushat Frye, 83–94. New York: Scribner's Sons, 1983.

Young, Davis A., and Ralph Stearley. *The Bible, Rocks, and Time: Geological Evidence for the Age of the Earth*. Downers Grove, IL: IVP Academic, 2008.